The American History Series

SERIES EDITORS
John Hope Franklin, *Duke University*
Abraham S. Eisenstadt, *Brooklyn College*

Arthur S. Link
Princeton University
GENERAL EDITOR FOR HISTORY

Robert L. Beisner
THE AMERICAN UNIVERSITY

From the Old Diplomacy to the New

1865–1900

SECOND EDITION

HARLAN DAVIDSON, INC.
ARLINGTON HEIGHTS, ILLINOIS 60004

Library of Congress Cataloging in Publication Data

Beisner, Robert L.
    From the old diplomacy to the new, 1865–1900.

    (The American history series)
    Bibliography: p.
    Includes index.
    1. United States—Foreign relations—1865–1898.
I. Title. II. Series.
E661.7.B44 1986   327.73   85-17649
ISBN 0-88295-833-X

Cover design: Roger Eggers. Cover illustration: *Rocky Mountain
News.*

Manufactured in the United States of America
91 90   4 5 6 7 TS

For John and Katharine

FOREWORD

Every generation writes its own history, for the reason that it sees the past in the foreshortened perspective of its own experience. This has certainly been true of the writing of American history. The practical aim of our historiography is to offer us a more certain sense of where we are going by helping us understand the road we took in getting where we are. If the substance and nature of our historical writing is changing, it is precisely because our own generation is redefining its direction, much as the generations that preceded us redefined theirs. We are seeking a newer direction, because we are facing new problems, changing our values and premises, and shaping new institutions to meet new needs. Thus, the vitality of the present inspires the vitality of our writing about our past. Today's scholars are hard at work reconsidering every major field of our history: its politics, diplomacy, economy, society, mores, values, sexuality, and status, ethnic, and race relations. No less significantly, our scholars are using newer modes of investigation to probe the ever-expanding domain of the American past.

Our aim, in this American History Series, is to offer the reader a survey of what scholars are saying about the central themes and issues of American history. To present these themes and issues, we have invited scholars who have made notable contributions to the respective fields in which they are writing. Each volume offers the reader a sufficient factual and narrative account for perceiving the larger dimensions of its particular subject. Addressing their respective themes, our authors have undertaken, moreover, to present the conclusions derived by the principal writers on these themes. Beyond that, the authors present their own conclusions about those aspects of their respective subjects that have been matters of difference and controversy. In effect, they have written not only about where the subject stands in today's historiography but also about where they stand on their subject. Each volume closes with an extensive critical essay on the writings of the major authorities on its particular theme.

The books in this series are designed for use in both basic and advanced courses in American history. Such a series has a particular utility in times such as these, when the traditional format of our American history courses is being altered to accommodate a greater diversity of texts and reading materials. The series offers a number of distinct advantages. It extends and deepens the dimensions of course work in American history. In proceeding beyond the confines of the traditional textbook, it makes clear that the study of our past is, more than the student might otherwise infer, at once complex, sophisticated, and profound. It presents American history as a subject of continuing vitality and fresh investigation. The work of experts in their respective fields, it opens up to the student the rich findings of historical inquiry. It invites the student to join, in major fields of research, the many groups of scholars who are pondering anew the central themes and problems of our past. It challenges the student to participate actively in exploring American history and to collaborate in the creative and rigorous adventure of seeking out its wider reaches.

John Hope Franklin

Abraham S. Eisenstadt

ACKNOWLEDGMENTS

I should like first to acknowledge the encouragement and friendly criticism of two history colleagues at The American University, Valerie French and Allan J. Lichtman. They have made the second edition of this book better, I hope, than its predecessor. A. S. Eisenstadt and John Hope Franklin painstakingly read and critiqued both editions. Maureen Trobec of Harlan Davidson, Inc., has been helpful throughout. Mary Beisner's reading of the first edition improved many a phrase, as did Robert Carola's.

Former students contributed greatly to the original conception of this book: Michael Roskin for urging me to look at Thomas S. Kuhn's paradigms; others—Wayne S. Knight, Richard Norment, and William Sweeney—for listening patiently and criticizing honestly.

Fellowships from The American University in 1970 and 1972 that freed me from summer teaching speeded up the first edition. I wish also to thank Julie Moran, who cheerfully took on the task of putting the first edition text on diskettes, a project funded by the College of Arts and Sciences of The American University. Few complete sentences from the first edition survived intact after my rewriting, but having the original text in such convenient form greatly smoothed the way to this book's completion.

I regret that the late Harlan Davidson, Sr., did not live to see this edition. Harlan above all was a publisher who genuinely loved good books, which "his" authors therefore have had extra reason to try writing.

Since the first edition of this book appeared, my children, John and Katharine, have faced in their own lives daunting challenges that have nothing to do with books. For their intelligence and great good cheer in meeting them—and for remaining undaunted—I dedicate this book to them, with my deepest gratitude for all the joy they have given me.

CONTENTS

Introduction

My purpose in this volume is not to provide a complete factual narrative of American foreign relations in the years 1865 to 1900. Instead, hoping that the reader already knows the details or is now absorbing them, I have concentrated on assessing recent scholarship in the field and offering new ways to look at the issues involved.

Students sometimes react to conflicting historical interpretations with puzzlement. I hope to help out in this book through discussions of the specific issues that have aroused controversy, such as the causes of the Spanish-American War, the annexation of the Philippines, and the promulgation of the Open Door policy. A strictly chronological narrative, however, would not adequately clarify some of the sharpest and most bewildering differences among historians. This book, therefore, opens with a chapter on the underlying circumstances, traditions, and ideas that shaped the conduct of United States diplomacy throughout the years 1865–1900, and on several knotty historiographical controversies that have divided its chroniclers.

The new way I propose to look at these years will, I hope, reconcile some earlier views usually thought to be in conflict. This interpretation first appears in Chapter Two, which otherwise discusses American foreign policy in the years from 1865 to 1889. Chapter Three contains an analysis of the fundamental change in policy that occurred in the late 1880s and early 1890s. Chapter Four deals with the early years (1889–97) of this new era and Chapter Five with its climax in the administration of William McKinley (1897–1901).

Clearly, around the year 1890 the United States entered on a more aggressive and expansionist phase in its diplomatic history and reached out into the world in an increasingly determined and deliberate fashion. This change did not occur overnight—we cannot suppose that a secretary of state rolled out of bed one morning, rubbed his eyes, and exclaimed, "This morning we are a great power!" Nor was the change total, for history is never so accommodating. But by the mid-nineties at the latest, American policymakers had begun to see foreign affairs from a new perspective, to confront the outer world with new assumptions and concerns, and to seek new objectives. One of the prime purposes of this book is to explain the nature of this change and the reasons it took place.

ONE

Underlying Themes and Issues

CIRCUMSTANTIAL GIVENS

The foundation of any nation's foreign policy includes certain "givens"—circumstances, conditions, institutions, beliefs, and attitudes—that guide its diplomacy toward some goals and away from others. These always-present factors define the perimeters of policy within which both dangers and opportunities are restricted. Especially important in the latter nineteenth century were six circumstantial and institutional "givens": conflict in Europe, economic developments, public opinion, the United States Senate, party politics, and the instruments of foreign affairs; and four influential traditions: the American Mission, isolationism, the Monroe Doctrine, and the Open Door.

Conflict in Europe

On occasion American policymakers have found their job made easier by conflicts among European states, a phenomenon described by Samuel F. Bemis as "America's Advantage from Europe's Distress." During the early years of the Republic the wars of the French Revolution and Napoleon tore Europe apart, leaving in their wreckage American diplomatic triumphs over distracted European powers. Even after Europe grew relatively more tranquil, Americans benefited from new tensions when they arose. Prussia's drive to unify Germany, for example, contributed to the withdrawal of French troops from Mexico in 1866–67. Russian denunciation of the Black Sea Treaty and the outbreak of the Franco-Prussian War in 1870 pushed Great Britain toward an amicable settlement of the *Alabama* controversy, which first arose during the Civil War. During the 1895–96 crisis that erupted over Venezuela's border with British Guiana, Britain again proved a weaker adversary to the United States than expected, this time because Britain was threatened by diplomatic isolation in Europe and a colonial rebellion in South Africa.

Economic Developments

An even more important "given" influencing foreign policy was America's rapid conversion to an industrial economy. Precisely how this influenced officials in Washington has been noisily debated by scholars, and this question will be examined later in the chapter. All agree, however, that the emergence of the United States as the world's leading producer of manufactured goods added significantly to its impact on world affairs, reduced Southern and rural domestic influence over American policy, alerted diplomats to the importance of promoting U.S. exports in foreign markets, and expanded the areas of the world in which Americans believed their national interests were involved.

Public Opinion

Although hard to measure, public opinion was a factor of fundamental domestic importance. Popular sentiment unquestionably played roles in prolonging the *Alabama* claims controversy, pushing the United States and Spain to the precipice of war in the 1870s, and toppling them over the brink in 1898. Public opinion killed President Grant's effort to annex Santo Domingo in 1870. It applied brakes to the rapprochement with Great Britain at the end of the century. Examples abound, but historians have never satisfactorily learned how to weigh the exact impact of public opinion on policymakers. Then, as now, officials could create "public opinion" from scratch or massage it into desired shape. Because of public ignorance and indifference, the government could often carry out a peripheral policy on the assumption that no opinion had developed on the matter. People who actually paid sustained attention to foreign affairs shifted in numbers and identity: one group might attend to British issues, another to Chinese, yet another to Cuban. And as Ernest R. May and others have pointed out, tiny elites in a few metropolitan centers dominated the foreign-policy opinions of thousands of followers. The political leader glancing over his shoulder to see if the "public" was following usually cared not about mass support but about the approval of a few acknowledged opinion makers and influential newspapers. On other occasions his backward glance might have been directed to the leaders of special interest and ethnic groups, whether steel manufacturers, grain exporters, Irish-Americans, or missionaries.

The United States Senate

Executive policymakers could not escape contending with Congress, and especially the Senate, whose members possessed a haughty institutional pride and certain exclusive constitutional prerogatives in declaring war, approving treaties, and confirming diplomatic appointments. In his novel *Democracy*, Henry Adams spoke of a government "of the people, by the people, for the Senate." He had in mind the body of men who, among other things, blocked the annexation of Santo Domingo, scrapped a long series of reciprocal trade agreements, rejected an arbitration agreement with Great Britain (the Olney-Pauncefote Treaty of 1897), nearly defeated the treaty concluding the Spanish-American War, and forced renegotiation of the pact (the first Hay-Pauncefote Treaty, 1900) clearing the way for exclusive American control of an isthmian canal. Many more accords never went beyond the negotiating table or never were submitted for ratification, because of anticipated Senate hostility.

Party Politics

Another constant was partisan politics, which affected presidents and secretaries of state just as much as congressmen. Republicans generally backed foreign policies more assertive than the Democrats supported. More to the point, one party always stood ready to harass and embarrass the other over foreign policy issues. Thus the egregious Benjamin F. Butler surprised few contemporaries in hoping that talks with Britain on the *Alabama* issue would collapse in a heap of recrimination, stirring up enough Anglophobia to ensure a GOP victory in the 1872 elections. On the other hand, the Grant administration believed that settling the *Alabama* issue offered a good way to outflank dissident Liberal Republicans. Yet Secretary of State Hamilton Fish almost wrecked the settlement by catering to public opinion and returning to divisive issues the British had thought were already in hand. Further examples of such partisanship also abound, as in Secretary of State James G. Blaine's scheming for an 1881 pan-American conference as a step to the presidency, the Republicans' defeating an important Canadian fisheries agreement in 1888 because Democratic officials had negotiated it, or President Cleveland's agreeing to the exclusion of Chinese immigrants because the voters of California demanded it. A more responsible treatment of foreign affairs began to emerge in the nineties, as we shall see, but the role of politics in diplomacy by no means disappeared. Foreign policy, not yet inextricably linked with "national security," could still be employed for domestic political objectives without great risk of rebuke. No one had yet coined the phrase "bipartisan foreign policy."

Instruments of Foreign Affairs

Those responsible for carrying out the nation's relations with other countries used the instruments of international power available to them: the diplomatic corps, the army, and the navy. American diplomats are discussed later in this chapter; it suffices to say that, with notable exceptions, U.S. diplomats during most of the era were clumsy amateurs at best. Even less impressive was the diminutive American army. Numbering around 28,000 men until the onset of the Spanish-American War, in 1890 it ranked about thirteenth in the world, smaller than Bulgaria's. Since most of its units were scattered about, chasing errant Indians, exploring mountain passes, or dredging river channels, the United States Army ranked even lower as a military force. This weakness was tolerable, even appropriate, so long as American policymakers had nothing too ambitious in mind. The outbreak of war in 1898, however, demanded speedy expansion, and by 1900 nearly 100,000 men wore the national colors. Even then, with 9,500 soldiers in Cuba and 61,000 fighting in the Philippine-American War, Washington was hard pressed to find a few thousand men for the international force raised in 1900 to suppress the Boxer Rebellion in China.

Given America's geographical setting and primary interests, in the late nineteenth century a good navy mattered more than a large army. But the vigorous Union navy had been dismantled after the Civil War, and its poor remnant often seemed as inadequate as the army in the years that followed. American actions in the Caribbean in the 1870s, for instance, could not overlook decrepit boilers that kept American warships from making more than 4½ of the 12 knots for which they were designed. In 1884, eleven other nations' navies put more vessels afloat than did the United States. Possibly more dangerous to their crews than any enemy, American ships were described the next year by the future secretary of the navy John D. Long as "an alphabet of floating wash-tubs."

Efforts to refurbish the navy began in the early eighties under the leadership of President Chester A. Arthur, Secretary of the Navy William E. Chandler, and Commodore Stephen B. Luce. Under their aegis Captain Alfred T. Mahan's bookish talents found a shoreside platform in the new Naval War College. A modest rebuilding program started, and it quickened in the 1890s. Though by 1898 the navy could easily outmatch Spain's ramshackle fleets, the glare of brilliant victories at Manila and off Cuban shores diverted attention from remaining weaknesses. As recently as 1894 a ship ordered to Nicaragua during the Corinto Affair (Chapter Four) had sunk ignominiously en route, and on the eve of war in 1898 the navy possessed only eight heavily armored ships, none of which met the European standard for "battleship."

Despite its shortcomings, the U.S. Navy at times played a conspicuous role in American diplomacy. In 1872, before naval communications were revolutionized by underwater telegraphic cables, Commander Richard W. Meade took it on himself to obtain American control of the Samoan harbor of Pago Pago (only to have the Senate reject his handiwork). Captain Robert W. Shufeldt's 1878 voyage along the coast of West Africa aroused American interest in that continent; four years later he inaugurated United States ties with Korea. As William R. Braisted has observed, "naval considerations were often determining factors in the formulation of the Far Eastern policies of the United States" (see the bibliographical essay at the end of the book).

That government officials, journalists, and the American people complacently tolerated such a flimsy array of diplomatic instruments, that they permitted minor commodores to take far-reaching diplomatic initiatives, suggests how little inclination existed in Gilded Age Washington to define and control a "foreign policy." More the rule than the exception until the 1890s, this vacuum in centralized policymaking marked a nation still lacking a coherent approach to international affairs.

AMERICAN
BELIEFS AND TRADITIONS

"Givens" of a circumstantial nature may have set the general boundaries of American foreign policy, but within those boundaries the specific directions of diplomacy were determined by beliefs and traditions that demanded little conscious thought or reflection. These beliefs and traditions were ingrained—"given" in the strictest sense of the word.

The American Mission

At the foundation was the belief that the American people possessed a special mission. They were destined not merely to inhabit the earth: they would create a free nation and a Way of Life (as it came to be called) better than any other in history. Since this concept made Americans feel inherently superior to all other peoples, it hardly mattered that Bulgaria's army outnumbered their own. What was a large army compared with a high calling? Woodrow Wilson would later recast this mission as an active duty to spread American principles and institutions to the rest of the world. Post–Civil War Americans, however, were content with a passive interpretation, holding that their only obligation was in providing an example for the rest of the world to emulate.

Even so, from the first the idea of mission carried the seed of an expansionist impulse. Partly for lack of ancient racial or ethnic ties to one another, Americans early on looked elsewhere for a source of national identity. They forged their bonds of unity from the ore of shared beliefs and experiences. To be an "American" was to believe in freedom, to live under the Constitution, to build railroads across the prairies, to conquer the wilderness. Being a Swede or a Russian had no application in, say, Cuba or China; being an "American," however, was a universalistic idea relevant everywhere. At first this missionary nationalism produced little more than a swaggering diplomatic posture, but as the nation increased in measurable power, Americans became more confident in their superiority over others. The imperialistic implications of the American Mission began to emerge.

Isolationism

This tradition, much misunderstood today, had an obvious meaning to Americans a century ago. At a time when the fastest ships afloat took 7½ days to get from New York to London and 120 to Hong Kong, Americans were ever mindful of their country's physical isolation from Europe and its imperial outposts. But isolation was more than a physical fact; it was a national goal. The American diplomat kept a distance from European power disputes and conducted U.S. affairs independently of European chancelleries as a prudent way to pursue selfish national interests. The American public relied on isolation as a prophylactic to prevent contamination of the American Experiment by decadent European mores and institutions.

Not that Americans could actually isolate themselves from the rest of the world. The U.S. maintained diplomatic ties and trade relations with many nations. It often cooperated with other powers in the Far East; it frequently asserted itself in the Western Hemisphere, especially in Central America and the Caribbean. As Selig Adler wrote in *The Isolationist Impulse: Its Twentieth Century Reaction* (1957), "our isolationist barricade had only one wall. We shut only our eastern door, for Americans marched out of their house in other directions." But the Founding Fathers' hope persisted that Americans could eschew power politics while *ideal* trading with anyone they liked. Thus, Secretary of State Thomas F. Bayard could declare in 1885: "So long as I am head of this Department, I shall not give myself the slightest trouble to thwart the small politics or staircase intrigues in Europe, in which we have not the slightest share or interest, and upon which I look with impatience and contempt."

The Monroe Doctrine

This operated as a kind of corollary to isolationism, for only a small step separated wanting European noninterference within the Western Hemisphere from insisting on it. Monroe's original statement in 1823 stipulated that Europeans should not reimpose their rule on already independent states in the hemisphere; it did not demand the liberation of remaining European colonies. Nevertheless, the doctrine contained an implicit call to eradicate all European influence in the area. Thus liberating Cuba ("Get the Spanish out"), or even annexing Canada ("Get the British out"), would represent nothing more than fitting ways to live up to the Monroe Doctrine.   *As An Excuse*

The Venezuela Crisis of 1895-96 first transformed the Monroe Doctrine from a timely policy for 1823 to a sacred principle for all time. Earlier, the United States had used the

doctrine selectively, winking at European incursions in the
hemisphere that seemed to do no real harm. When Washington did resist such incursions, it rarely mentioned the Monroe Doctrine. In the years 1865–1900, however, the idea of
eliminating any *dangerous* European presence from the
hemisphere emerged as an emotion-arousing tenet of American foreign policy, particularly in the nineties.

The Open Door

Long before the Open Door notes of 1899–1900, Americans had used the phrase and recognized the importance of
the policy it described. Decades before the depression of the
mid-nineties caused a panicky rush to export surplus industrial products, American merchants had sought an open door
for trade. These businessmen included exporters, who
wanted low and nondiscriminatory tariffs levied on their
goods (as well as other "open door" arrangements); impor-
ters, bent on promoting an atmosphere friendly to international trade; and shippers, who would benefit from open
ports regardless of whose goods were carried in their vessels. Even though most Americans thought of international
commerce as a private matter, statesmen from John Jay to
John Hay well knew that one of their main jobs was keeping
an open door for American businessmen.

CONFLICTING INTERPRETATIONS

Few historians would differ with the discussion thus far. But
scholars have offered many conflicting interpretations of
U.S. foreign relations from 1865 to 1900. The remainder of
this chapter examines four of the most important general issues dividing scholarly opinion. Though these issues overlap
at several points, for the sake of clarity we can separate

them into: (1) the Continuity Issue; (2) the Economic Issue; (3) the Semantic Issue; and (4) the Deliberateness Issue.

⟶ 1865 − 1900 Era

The Continuity Issue

The question is whether American imperialism in the 1890s represented a logical climax to the era preceding it or a break with the past. Until the end of the 1950s most historians held to a "discontinuity" thesis. For twenty-five years *Disc.* after the Civil War, they argued, Americans were too busy rebuilding, pioneering the West, and stoking the new furnaces of industry to pay much attention to foreign affairs. Though the department of state's doors stayed open, diplomats sought little more than keep the United States out of mischief and protect its most obvious and nearby interests. Some Americans wanted even less action, and these included the congressman who in an 1870s budget debate called for the United States to close down all but its London and Berlin legations. Then, in this view of the period, around 1890 such intellectuals as Josiah Strong, Brooks Adams, and Alfred T. Mahan suddenly began thinking imperialist thoughts, the navy feverishly set to laying hulls for a new fleet, manufacturers started clamoring for foreign markets, and warmongering sensationalists seized the editorial offices of American newspapers. In short order, the United States bullied Chile over a barroom brawl, angled to annex Hawaii and Samoa, forced a showdown with Britain over Venezuela's border, and finally stripped Spain of her overseas empire.

For some "discontinuity" historians, the outburst of the nineties marked the mere debut of a new entry in the ranks of imperial powers; for others, the events of 1898–99 were an aberration, quickly followed by a renewed distaste for colonialism. *Split* All these historians, however, concur that the Spanish-American War and colonial annexations represented a sharp turn from the preceding era when, as Henry Cabot

Lodge complained in 1889, "our relations with foreign nations . . . fill[ed] but a slight place in American politics, and excite[ed] generally only a languid interest."

Most scholarly historians today adhere to a "continuity" thesis, particularly those who emphasize the economic foundations of post–Civil War diplomacy. The most persuasive case is made in *The New Empire: An Interpretation of American Expansion, 1860–1898* (1963) by Walter LaFeber, who treats the period as a seamless epoch dominated by America's transformation from an agrarian to an industrial nation. Capitalist industrialization brought in its train recurrent economic depressions, blamed at the time on overproduction. Unless the growing surplus of goods could be marketed abroad, American society would face falling profits and burgeoning unemployment. Radical nostrums would gain popular force, jeopardizing middle-class democratic government itself. To prevent this outcome, one administration after another from Lincoln to McKinley (though more urgently later in the period) deliberately wielded foreign policy as an instrument designed to eliminate this destabilizing surplus.

A significant break in continuity involved tactics rather than long-term objectives, according to LaFeber. This shift involved a change from the traditional assumption that America's economic goals could be achieved without the annexation of colonies, to the belief that imperialist solutions would be required after all. Temporary in duration, this tactical shift stemmed from several causes: the shattering depression of 1893–97, which made acquiring new foreign markets more urgent than ever; the carving up of China and soaring tariff walls of Europe, both of which threatened previously open markets; and the course of events in the Spanish-American War itself. Although tactics might alter, however, the strategic objective remained the same: to sell abroad the surplus caused by "overproduction" in the American economy.

Nearly all historians have detected some discontinuity in

this period. But we must ask: How much discontinuity? How significant is it? Historians can discover chronological watersheds of all sorts depending on what they are looking for. Events that appear momentous to one scholar may be totally ignored by another. A "discontinuity" historian who wants to demonstrate the suddenness of the imperialist surge of 1898–1900 will note that as recently as 1895 Secretary of State Walter Q. Gresham complacently remarked that the Sino-Japanese War "endangers no policy of the United States in Asia." A "continuity" historian, on the other hand, can counter by showing how far Gresham's chief, President Cleveland, approached hostilities with Spain several years prior to the supposed watershed of 1898. Yet another historian, impressed by the complexity of the issue, could argue that almost nothing new happened in U.S. policy toward Europe and Africa in the 1865–1900 era; that a major change in relations with Latin America occurred in 1895, if not earlier; and that U.S. relations with East Asia shifted drastically, but not until 1898. Because these variations seem endless, as well as contradictory, a new chronological framework and new approach to the continuity issue will be offered later in this book.

The Economic Issue

Although much of the discussion above concerns economic factors in late-nineteenth-century American foreign policy, the issue deserves separate attention. For many years historians followed the view of Julius W. Pratt's *Expansionists of 1898: The Acquisition of Hawaii and the Spanish Islands* (1936), which demonstrated strong business opposition to waging war against Spain, and works of other scholars who believed they had found the prime causes of the 1898 war in Social Darwinist ideology, yellow journalism, popular frenzy, and spineless leadership. All these writers tended to discount the impact of economics on American policy. Beginning in the early 1960s, however, an economic perspective on the subject gained influence, spearheaded by the works of Walter LaFeber and William A. Williams. Their distinction in offering the only general interpretation encompassing the full sweep of the period 1865 to 1900 added to their persuasiveness.

An economic interpretation of American expansionism goes back at least to 1902, when the Englishman John Hobson argued in *Imperialism* that the origins of the imperial impulse resided in moneylenders' efforts to find profitable new regions for investing their surplus capital. But the idea that J. P. Morgan got the United States ensconced in Manila with his excess profits has always been too much to swallow. Stanley Lebergott noted in a 1980 article that only 1 percent of total American investment from 1869 to 1897 went abroad; and historians have long been aware that the United States was a net borrower of capital until World War I. Recent accounts, therefore, have instead identified the drive to increase sales of goods in foreign markets as the impetus to American imperialism. Industrialization had led to a piling up of surpluses. Unless they were disposed of abroad, businessmen and leaders in Washington would face grim choices: either production cuts that would reduce profits, throw thousands out of work, and stir social unrest; or, worse still, a redistribution of wealth on a scale permitting workers to buy the surplus products themselves—in short, a form of socialism.

Given the alternative, U.S. officials saw the wisdom of helping businessmen sell their surplus abroad. Policymakers began shaping diplomacy to achieve this economic objective. Although erratic at first, their efforts gained in system as time passed, especially as business effectively supplanted agriculture as the dominant political influence in Washington. The most urgent focus on foreign markets came in the climacteric of the mid-nineties, when a wrenching panic and depression occurred just as historian Frederick Jackson Turner pronounced the vanishing of the safety-valve frontier of free land. Unnerved by these blows, haunted by fears of economic stagnation or staccato crises, statesmen and businessmen pitched headlong into an aggressive search for new markets as a way out.

Latin America and the Far East looked liked the most promising areas for expansion. Administrations long depicted as epitomes of aimlessness and mediocrity, so the argument goes, actually laid the platform of the "new empire" through tariff reform, reciprocal-trade agreements, armed interventions against revolutions, and hemispheric harassment of European poachers—all to maintain and expand American exports. Because the process culminated in war and colonial annexations did not mean American leaders wanted it that way; it meant that in 1898 and 1899 they saw no other way to get what they did want.

This interpretation avoids the crude sort of revisionism that blames American imperialism on a Wall Street conspiracy. Its defenders instead contend that American foreign policy was the product of an openly reached consensus of businessmen, politicians, and intellectuals. These men should not be seen as ideological colonialists, but as moderates who would have preferred to settle for a few island bases and a navy designed to protect the trade of American merchants. They wanted an "informal empire" created by the demand for good American products, not a formal empire seized by the weapons of war.

Historians not convinced by this argument were quick to point out the apparently meager results of commercial diplomacy. Although U.S. exports to China rose from $3 million in 1890 to $15 million in 1900, the latter represented only 1.1 percent of total American exports, hardly an imperial share. Foreign trade absorbed but a small slice of the gross national product in the late nineteenth century, and most of that commerce was with Canada and Europe. In 1900, for example, 44 percent of all U.S. exports went to Great Britain and France, a mere 3 percent to China and Japan. Moreover, critics observed, farm products, not the surplus of overbuilt factories, still accounted for the bulk of American exports to the very end of the century.

"Informal empire" historians, as well as others, are not without responses to these criticisms. American trade statistics of the time, for example, are not so modest as critics suggest. The United States, which accounted for less than 4 percent of the world's exports of manufactured goods at the beginning of the 1890s, was responsible for 9.8 percent by 1899, a jump of more than 100 percent in less than a decade. Moreover, even modest increases in exports might separate profit and loss for a particular company, prosperity and stagnation for the economy at large. Exports to certain regions, though small in the global picture, loomed large for some industries—almost half of all American cotton textile exports found their way to China in the late nineties.

Defenders of the foreign-markets thesis also argue that proving their case does not require massive economic results, but evidence that American leaders *believed* promoting exports was imperative, and *believed* in the shimmering China market.

William A. Williams has directly confronted the continuing vitality of trade in farm commodities in *Roots of the Modern American Empire* (1969). In 1869 Americans earned as much by exporting animal tallow and butter as iron and steel. As late as 1880, agricultural staples constituted 84.3 percent of the dollar value of all U.S. exports. Williams's view is that the drive for foreign markets was begun by Jefferson's yeoman farmers. For decades afterward, wheat farmers, cattle-raisers, cotton planters, dairymen, food processors, and their allies advocated a foreign policy aimed at finding markets for farm products. The significance of the 1890s lay in the rise to power of urban ("metropolitan") leaders, who captured export policy for themselves and turned it to the needs of an industrial economy. Williams's book, unique in the field, attempts valiantly to absorb agriculture within the foreign-markets thesis. His focus on ordinary farmers and their spokesmen instead of the industrial-political elite also places renewed emphasis on the popular roots of American imperialism.

The economic approach to American foreign policy offers a valuable framework to the student of the late nineteenth century; its findings are essential in explaining some specific episodes. Nonetheless, the argument has too many shortcomings to provide a key to the whole period. As we will see, it is simplistic to suppose that an entire generation of policymakers toiled away at precise, rational calculations of the nation's economic interests. Moreover, the evidence includes too many discrepancies to allow an endorsement of the economic interpretation.

Many Americans actually shrugged aside economic issues, or they believed that politics were more important when shaping U.S. diplomacy. When Secretary of State Fish in 1870 alerted the Grant cabinet to an opportunity for expanded American trade and influence in Hawaii, he was met with total silence and "the subject [was] dropped." Throughout the 1870s and eighties the United States knowingly jeopardized trade with China in response to xenophobes' mistrust of Chinese immigrants, especially in California, the state that might have gained most from more commerce with East Asia. Job competition and racial tensions exceeded foreign markets in importance. In 1884 the Arthur administration joined the Berlin conference on the future of the Congo, expecting commercial benefits for the United States; but in 1885 the new Cleveland government took the Berlin treaty out of the Senate's hands, thus preserving American isolation from big power affairs, a tradition more important than the prospects of foreign trade. Did President Benjamin Harrison (Chapter Four) shake a mailed fist at Chile in 1891–92 to open markets for Connecticut locomotives, or to avenge an insult to the American uniform and exert leverage against British influence in a Latin republic? In fact, patriotic fever and fear of a European play in the hemisphere counted more in the president's mind than profit and loss sheets. Historians have cited James G. Blaine's vain attempt in 1881 to arrange a pan-American conference as a pioneering venture in market expansionism. But according to Russell H. Bastert, the secretary of state was prompted by "a mixture of many motives," mostly the presidential bug, and "probably least of all economic" considerations. Similarily, Paul S. Holbo has shown that Grover Cleveland tried to reduce tariff levels in the nineties not to pull the nation out of depression through increased foreign trade but to fulfill campaign promises. He was more impressed by his party's low-tariff traditions and consumers' anger at paying high prices for family necessities than by the recommendations of exports-minded businessmen. Despite the calamitous depression, despite a "consensus" on the urgency of trade expansion, Congress quashed reciprocity agreements with Spain (for Cuba and Puerto Rico), Brazil, the Central American States, the British West Indies, Austria-Hungary, and Germany. Apparently, America's legislators had not gotten the word.

One reason officials felt they could treat foreign trade so cavalierly was the bad example set by businessmen themselves. Expansionist Brooks Adams grumbled about their "failure . . . to act intelligently and aggressively" in overseas emporiums. American exporters performed ineptly, even sloppily, marketing inferior and poorly packaged products. They shipped inappropriate goods (cheese to Holland), forfeited goodwill with unsafe products (tainted food, dangerous dyes in leather), and confounded customers with poor timing (furs for Canada in July). They relied on incompetent or negligent agents. In China, where commercial hopes were supposedly highest of all near the end of the century, the problem was particularly bad. From the time of the Civil War to the mid-nineties, one American mercantile house after another cut back its business or pulled out of China altogether. Throughout Asia U.S. manufacturers paid scant attention to what people actually wanted to buy, despite American consular officers' pleas that they adapt their goods to the markets at hand. American merchants approached Latin American markets just as lackadaisically. Little wonder that former diplomat Eugene Schuyler in 1886 denounced "the inertia and obstinacy of American manufacturers."

It is misleading, therefore, to picture a unified business community, backed by a determined state, striving without stint to break into the markets of Asia and Latin America. Most exporters still regarded trade as a matter between businessmen and distrusted the government. Even the smaller firms that William Becker has shown were most eager for help were of two minds about having politicians involved. More typically, businessmen wanted officials to concentrate on keeping foreigners out of the home market by maintaining America's tariff wall, a strategy calculated to stimulate exports neither in theory nor in practice. Protectionist sentiment held firm from the 1860s to the 1890s; by the 1880s not a single free-trader remained in the Senate from the purportedly expansionist Republican Party. The annual congressional debates on the tariff, Paul S. Holbo insists, aroused far more passion than those on foreign trade, the debaters spending their strength arguing about jobs for workers, relief for consumers, and such abstractions as "Americanism" and "Jeffersonianism"—not export strategy. Nearly all those businessmen who did aggressively seek foreign sales kept their eyes on proven markets in Canada and Europe, and focused on the fallow regions of Asia and Latin America only after 1900.

The conduct of officials and businessmen fails to support the interpretation of late-nineteenth century American foreign policy presented by "foreign-markets" historians. That the United States government should knowingly plan and skillfully carry out a farsighted economic diplomacy contradicts what we know about American "policymakers." Until no earlier than the nineties, most U.S. officials were amateurish and maladroit in their diplomacy, ignorant of other societies and their affairs, and more likely to react to outside events in habitual ways than to come up with fresh policies. Behavior, not occasional rhetoric, is the crucial test. What did presidents and secretaries of state actually do through most of the years from 1865 to 1900? They occasionally paraded interest in the expansion of foreign markets, of course, but usually seemed unconcerned. The men they sent to foreign posts, usually products of the spoils system, were often unfit to hold any public office, let alone to execute a grand economic program. And Congress? It raised the tariff ever higher, scorned the idea of reciprocity treaties, sacrificed quality in the diplomatic service on the altar of thrift, and regularly rejected proposals to establish a professional consular service. Most of all, members of Congress could be counted on to put partisan concerns above good relations with other nations.

As to businessmen, they remained preoccupied with exploiting the growing home market and, when they did enter the export game, continued to look to the traditional and nonimperialistic markets of Canada and Europe. Tables I and II illustrate both points.

TABLE I   United States Exports as Percentage of Estimated Gross National Product in Selected Years

Year	Total Exports	Pct. of GNP (est.)
1874	$ 606,000,000	8.1%
1884	752,600,000	7.1
1889	762,700,000	6.4
1891	909,800,000	6.7
1893	862,300,000	6.5
1895	807,500,000	5.8
1897	1,051,000,000	7.5
1899	1,227,000,000	6.9
1900	1,394,500,000	7.5

TABLE II   Exports to Canada and Europe Compared with Exports to Asia and Latin America

Year	Exports to Canada and Europe	Pct. of Total	Exports to Asia and Latin America	Pct. of Total
1875	$ 494,000,000	86.1%	$ 72,000,000	12.5%
1885	637,000,000	85.8	87,000,000	11.7
1895	681,000,000	84.3	108,000,000	13.4
1900	1,135,000,000	81.4	200,000,000	14.3

Tables compiled from information in *Historical Statistics of the United States*, 1960; U.S. Department of Commerce, *Long Term Growth, 1860-1965*, 1966; National Bureau of Economic Research, *Trends in the American Economy in the Nineteenth Century*, 1960.

The economic interpretation cannot be ignored. We must blend it with other views, however, to create a useful synthesis. We have long been aware that foreign trade and other economic issues left visible traces in the history of American diplomacy. Unfortunately, scholars have too often focused on economics to the neglect of other factors and have overlooked the political and ideological facets of economic issues. Agile politicians have never lacked talent at bending economic issues to their own purposes. David Healy in *US Expansionism: The Imperialist Urge in the 1890s* (1970) contends that statesmen in pursuit of national power and prestige often scattered "markets" buzzwords through their speeches to grab the loyalty of voters who seemed more interested in dollars and cents than glory. Even more common than politicians who manipulated economic, political, and ideological issues were those who never dreamed of separating them. Perhaps they hoped to enlarge American political influence in China during the 1890s, but for what purpose if not to open doors for U.S. exports? Conversely, a greater economic role in China meant greater power for the United States throughout the Far East, something Washington did not find difficult to fathom. Both the "profit" and "power" oriented, Robert Wiebe writes in *The Search for Order, 1877–1920* (1967), wished to achieve international stability. "The apostles of power . . . saw investment, like trade, merely as one piece in an elaborate game."

In short, most Americans merged economics into a broader vision. Not only did profits and power combine to raise both standards of living and status among nations, but Americans detected even more special dimensions in foreign trade. For, as James A. Field, Jr., and others have noted, they viewed trade not just as a source of profits, but also a wellspring of social enlightenment, moral improvement, and international peace. That economics played an important role in late-nineteenth-century American foreign policy is undeniable. That its role was subtle and complex should also be clear.

The Semantic Issue

A perennial source of confusion, but one that need not detain us long, is the word "imperialism" as applied to American diplomacy from 1865 to 1900. Most Americans, including historians, have narrowly construed the word to apply only to the formal annexation and control of foreign territories and peoples. They often spurn the word even when American actions clearly fit this narrow definition. Seizing the Southwest from Mexico, for example, was not "imperialistic," because the territory had been "uninhabited" (save for tens of thousands of Indians and Mexicans) and was eventually incorporated as states into the Union. Nor did the annexation of Puerto Rico meet the test, since the local populace did not resist the takeover; nor was it "imperialistic" to annex the Philippines, where natives did fight vigorously for independence, because after laying down their arms they were treated benevolently and finally let go in 1946. Theodore Roosevelt spoke from this lexicon of denial at the turn of the century in asserting that "there is nothing even remotely resembling 'imperialism' or 'militarism' in the present development of . . . policy. . . .'' Such patriotic touchiness distorts the clear intent of language and causes patriotic Americans to deny the imperialistic realities of their past. Radical critics, on the other hand, have vulgarized ''imperialism'' by stretching it beyond recognition and by making the word almost useless in rational discourse. What can the word possibly mean when it is pasted as a label everywhere Americans have invested dollars or foreigners drink Coca Cola?

Since the word ''imperialism'' often generates more heat than light, many historians have been striving to define their terms more clearly. Marilyn B. Young, for instance, distinguishes between ''annexationists, mild or extreme,'' and those who ''advocated expanding foreign markets through forceful diplomatic representation, the reform of the consular service, and the construction of an isthmian canal.'' The ''economic school'' historians go to great lengths to note the differences among varying *isms*, usually arguing that most Americans were not ''colonialists'' who wanted to govern other peoples, but ''expansionists,'' ''open door expansionists,'' ''informal imperialists,'' or ''anticolonial imperialists.'' In one remarkable sentence Thomas J. McCormick has rung all the changes: ''Paradoxically, American expansion was designed in part to serve an anti-imperial purpose of preventing the colonization of China and thus preserving her open door market penetration: *the imperialism of anti-imperialism* ('neo-colonialism' in today's parlance).''

Such an eruption of terms suggests that a single set of definitions is not likely to please everyone; it also suggests the need to use the language of this issue both clearly and flexibly. Part of the semantic problem lies in neglecting to notice that, unsurprisingly, varying labels have been applied to different kinds of ''imperialists.'' At least six species of *Imperialistus americanus* (along with many hybrids) were at large among the fauna of late-nineteenth-century America:

(1) The Market Expansionist, who wanted nothing more than to empty the warehouse of America's productive surplus; (2) The Market Expansionist, subspecies A, who wanted to buttress export campaigns with an up-to-date navy, and to strengthen the navy by acquiring island "dots" and "points" for harbors, coaling stations, and repair facilities; (3) The Market Expansionist, subspecies B, who would accept the burden of direct colonial rule over other peoples, but only if maintaining influence in strategically important areas demanded it; (4) The Power Politician, who hailed the rising international power of the United States, wished to see the ascent continue for its own sake, and to that end countenanced using an array of instruments, including commercial diplomacy and colonialism; (5) The Colonialist, who, as an enthusiast for governing and civilizing "lesser breeds," sought to bring them the Word of God and to initiate them in the wondrous workings of Anglo-Saxon political institutions; and (6) The Wild Jingo who, like Benjamin F. Butler, would urge the United States to expand "so far north that wandering Esquimau will mistake the flashings of the midnight sun reflected from our glorious flag for the scintillations of an aurora borealis." Allan Nevins once dubbed an earlier phase of this spirit "Davy Crockett spread-eaglism."

The Deliberateness Issue

Was American foreign policy from 1865 to 1900 made in a deliberate fashion, carefully thought out and systematically executed by men who knew what they were doing; or was it passive, reactive, and haphazardly administered by officials who lacked both reliable information and conscious policy designs? Although most historians understand that uncontrollable events prevent any government, despite the best intentions, from acting in a uniformly intelligent and methodical fashion, they often part company in how they answer this question. The "foreign-markets" historians normally portray American officials as expert and rational, as do a few scholars eager for other reasons to rescue the late nineteenth century from stereotypes of venality and mediocrity. Many other historians, for assorted reasons, favor the alternative view. Our own answer to this question will be doubly significant: both influencing how we visualize the American diplomatic terrain of the period and, as we shall see later, pointing the way toward a fresh interpretation of the diplomatic shifts of the 1890s.

The market-expansion thesis, already discussed, presupposes conscious purpose on the part of policymakers. Other examples of deliberateness in U.S. diplomacy, apart from the commercial interpretation, also deserve attention. William H. Seward, secretary of state from 1861 to 1869, had a profoundly expansionist vision of America's future and elaborated both domestic and diplomatic schemes to bring it about. His successor, Hamilton Fish, well informed and adept at bureaucratic infighting, performed skillfully in juggling three major issues—the attempted annexation of the Dominican Republic, civil war in Cuba, and the *Alabama* claims—and resolving them all to his satisfaction (Chapter Two). Though James G. Blaine's foreign policy usually smacked more of expediency than deliberation, his 1881 description of why the United States should forge closer ties with Hawaii shows a bent for the large view.

Taking San Francisco as the commercial center on the western slope, a line drawn northwesterly to the Aleutian group marks our Pacific border almost to the confines of Asia. A corresponding line drawn southwesterly from San Francisco to Honolulu, marks the natural limit of the ocean belt within which our trade with the oriental countries must flow, and is, moreover, the direct line of communication between the United States and Australasia. Within this line lies the commercial domain of our western coast.

In the early nineties President Benjamin Harrison clearly understood the interlocking ties among the naval, commercial and diplomatic elements of foreign policy. And William McKinley, long regarded as an amiable weather vane, now draws regard from scholars as an able president and steward of a systematic foreign policy.

Some regions of the world inspired more consistent and coherent policies than others. In Latin America one administration after another worked to cut back European influence, promote the peaceable settlement of regional disputes, expand sales of American goods, and secure U.S. control of a future isthmian canal. China, too, tended to call forth unusual deliberateness in United States policymaking, especially at the end of the century.

All of which is not really so impressive considering how many American officials were unsophisticated in world affairs and more chaotic than systematic in their work. And able or not, American diplomatic officials normally waited inertly until an external stimulus of calamitous proportions forced them to come up with a suitable American response.

Despite sporadic gestures toward reform—and with some happy exceptions—the consular service consisted largely of time-serving functionaries, party hacks, bumptious fools, and petty corruptionists. In office, many attempted little beyond complaining about their meager furniture allowance and the condition in which their predecessors had left their quarters. The state department sent consuls to their posts with minimal and uniform instructions, whether they were destined for Caracas, Hamburg, Winnipeg, or Kobe. An 1872 report by a special inspector of consular officials in Asia and South America concluded that "not a single consulate [had] a complete set of record-books . . . as required," and that "almost every consulate had some defects . . . owing to the incompetency, low habits, and vulgarity of some of its officers during the endless round of evils" caused by rapid turnover of personnel. "Abuses had been committed in the collection of fees; in the exercise of judicial powers; in the adjustment of the business affairs of American citizens; in the settlement, where permitted, of the estates of intestate American citizens dying abroad; . . . and issuing illegal passports; . . . [and] in taxing Chinese emigrants"; but the worst "iniquity" was "defrauding the government and grasping gains from various outside sources."

Aside from such able men as John A. Kasson, Charles Francis Adams, and John Hay, American ministers (the rank of ambassador was not used until 1893) all too often earned more shame than respect for their country. In an era when foreign envoys could still leave their mark on important events, what can be said of a government that employed such men as Lewis D. Campbell, who, as minister to republican Mexico, wouldn't budge in 1867 from his New Orleans "headquarters" to deliver a plea for the life of Emperor Maximilian; or the amazing Rumsey Wing of Kentucky, sent by Grant at the age of twenty-seven to Ecuador, which he promptly urged the United States to annex, where he attempted to assassinate the British ambassador, and where he finally expired from delirium tremens and fever; or Charles E. DeLong, who mailed misspelled and ungrammatical dispatches to Secretary Fish and careened at full speed in his carriage through Tokyo streets, fondling the pistol sticking out of his belt and cracking a whip at astonished pedestrians; or peg-legged Dan Sickles, sent to Spain in the 1870s, who purportedly made love to the exiled Queen Regent and came close to making war during the Cuban civil war by using the mails to tell Washington of news promising peace but the cable to hurry along information of conflict? Egypt demanded the recall of Ben Butler's nephew as U.S. consul general, accusing him of drunkenness, buying slave wenches, and joining others in a wild shooting spree. One American consul in Mexico moonlighted by smuggling, another offended local mores by living with a prostitute. A U.S. newspaper in 1881 described Washington's minister to Peru as "grossly ignorant of the elementary principles of international law, and completely indifferent to the decorum of diplomatic intercourse." For years Brazil complained about the low-grade American representatives sent to Rio de Janeiro, none as outrageous as James Watson Webb, a "swindler" whose extortionate conduct in the 1860s was so bad that Congress compensated the Brazilians from the U.S. Treasury. Little wonder that the *New York Daily Tribune* in 1886 urged an experiment to see how high American diplomats could fly in balloons "without disgracing themselves and their country."

Irresponsible and incompetent officials are only part of the picture. Absence of clear policy permeated American diplomacy. In Europe, U.S. diplomats composed dispatches that ignored the continent's shifting alliances and recurrent crises. The "Eastern Question," so worrisome to European chancelleries in the seventies and eighties, failed to disturb the slumbers of American diplomats. Sandra C. Taylor has shown that Americans in Japan wanted Washington to support a greater role for Tokyo in Asia; they "had no following in the State Department, which, however, had no alternate policy ideas regarding Japan either." Even in the nineties, the United States often acted passively in the Far East, refusing a European bid to join in mediating the Sino-Japanese War (1894-95), snubbing its minister to China when he advocated a more forward policy, and offering a deaf ear to American businessmen who complained of being cheated out of chances to build railroads in the Middle Kingdom. Not until 1899 did the United States take the initiative in China, and then John Hay remarked on the difficulty of figuring out exactly what the government's view was on Chinese matters. Even close to home, Washington defaulted by insisting in 1877 that its minister to Mexico City decide whether to recognize the new Diaz regime. Especially when we recall that the day-to-day preoccupations of American diplomatic officials usually turned to protecting a meddlesome missionary in Turkey or holding talks on an extradition treaty with Russia, rather than administering a "policy" or announcing a major "decision," we will avoid exaggerating the deliberateness and consistency of post–Civil War American diplomacy.

Some Americans, of course, kept up on world affairs and advocated forceful policies. But such men—whether diplomats, naval officers, businessmen, or missionaries—usually operated on their own hook. Far ahead of their government, which responded infrequently if ever to their suggestions, they occasionally secured significant advantages for the United States. But these were often sanctioned after the fact and then only reluctantly; other advances were allowed to lapse through official indifference and inaction in Washington. Observing that diplomatic initiatives usually originated elsewhere, Robert Wiebe has written that American "foreign relations were composed of incidents, not policies—a number of distinct events, not sequences that moved from a source toward a conclusion." This began to change in the 1890s, however, when the passivity and drift of American foreign policy began to give way to more deliberateness and consistency. We must now turn to this change and the reasons for its appearance.

Ad-Hoc
Reactionary
Tackle Diplomacy

TWO

Old Paradigm Policy, 1865–1889

PARADIGMS AND DIPLOMACY

Historians have long noticed that in the fabric of late-nineteenth-century American foreign policy a few patterns stand out boldly against a background of somber hues and random traceries. These patterns, visible to any observer, represent the era's most important developments: a growing American domination of the Caribbean, the beginning of a

32

continuous U.S. interest and presence in East Asia, the ac- } Debate
quisition of an extraterritorial empire, and the emergence of
the United States as a world power. But, as we have seen,
authorities have sharply disagreed on the chronology of
these developments, the importance of economic factors in
bringing them about, and the purposefulness of the government in shaping these new patterns of foreign policy.

We may be able to resolve some disputes by recognizing
that something quite _different_ began to appear in U.S. diplomacy about 1890—the threads in the tapestry, though still
intertwined, began to sort themselves out and reach in new
directions. The something that happened in the nineties was
a major shift in the manner of thinking about and exe- } Develop
cuting American foreign policy: the old reactive, unsyste-
matic conduct of U.S. foreign relations was replaced by
the making of a real "policy" in international affairs and its
more-or-less systematic execution. Thus, hypothetically
speaking, while a secretary of state in 1880 would probably
have reacted separately and disjointedly to events in Big
Mexico, Canada, and China, his successor in 1900 would plan
more likely have anticipated the need for decision before
events overtook him, pondered the events in a framework
aimed at advancing a general foreign policy, and then acted
accordingly.

This is not to say that American foreign policy under-
went a total transformation in the decade before 1900; it did,
however, change remarkably in some respects and actually
began changing as early as the late 1880s. We do not need
new data as much as a fresh analytical tool to explain these
changes, refine some old interpretations, and reconcile views
that now seem in conflict. Such a tool is available in the
"paradigm."

A "paradigm" is simply a model or pattern, but the
word takes on special meaning in Thomas S. Kuhn's path-
breaking book on the history of science, _The Structure of
Scientific Revolutions_ (2d ed., 1970)—a meaning adaptable

to the field of diplomatic history. Kuhn uses "paradigm" to refer to an "entire constellation of beliefs, values, techniques," axioms, and theories shared by a community of scientists at any particular time in history. While the belief that the sun revolved around the earth set one paradigm, the Copernican "revolution" established another. Physicists who viewed electricity as a fluid carried out experiments and talked to their peers within the framework of one paradigm; twentieth century physics labs operate within another. A paradigm determines the contemporary definitions of scientific "truth" and respectable scientific activity (though astrology is not now deemed a respectable science, it once was). It mandates correct methodology in a scientific field and produces the "expectations" of its practitioners. The paradigm serves as a filter for the perception of evidence, defining the way a scientist sees the "objective" natural world around him.

When widespread disagreements divide scientists about the fundamentals of their field, no paradigm is in effect. Conversely, with a paradigm in force, scientists accept the basic principles of their field as givens (they share "mental sets") and are therefore free to focus on solving derivative puzzles in a kind of "mopping-up" operation, such as filling in gaps in the periodic table of elements or, as Kuhn has elsewhere written, figuring out the "topographical detail on a map whose main outlines are available in advance. . . ." At such times scientific communication is quick and simple, since important words and formulas need only be stated to be instantly recognized. A scientific paradigm is like "an accepted judicial decision in the common law," a general principle requiring only "further articulation and specification. . . .' Just as judges can briefly cite a major precedent and then get on with the work at hand, so scientists can allude to "velocity" or "energy"—without fear of being misunderstood—and then concentrate on solving the special problem facing them.

Paradigms, Kuhn argues, do not usually follow one another gradually and incrementally, but abruptly. Scientists tend to remain stubbornly loyal to a paradigm—it is, after all, their definition of the real world—even when faced by multiple discoveries contradicting it. These violated expectations ("anomalies") are first shrugged off as quirky accidents, or by definition simply ruled out of order, but if they appear often enough to throw doubt on "normal" science and accepted procedures, the anomalies will produce "incommensurable ways of seeing the world and of practicing science in it"—in short, a scientific crisis. At this juncture, a new theory capable of explaining the anomalies will arise, recasting them as normal occurrences, and when enough scientists concur, will take over rather suddenly as the new paradigm. With a new paradigm in effect, the former "anomalies" are integrated as comfortable regularities within the new way of explaining things, while some old aspects of the science that had seemed unproblematical become question marks. A "scientific revolution" having occurred, scientists will in a manner of speaking be "responding to a different world."

I propose an adaptation of Kuhn's thesis as an aid in explaining the "revolution" in American foreign policy in the 1890s. Readers should not take the analogy to scientific change literally. The second of the two diplomatic "paradigms" discussed below, for example, neither succeeded the first instantaneously nor ever replaced it entirely. Compared with descriptions of clear-cut scientific revolutions, the picture of American diplomatic change appears rather muddy; instead of materializing full-blown overnight, the new paradigm gradually grew in strength and significance throughout the 1890s. And from approximately 1888 to 1895 the factors causing the old paradigm to topple are at times hard to distinguish from the traits of its successor.

Nonetheless, an analogy need not be exact to be helpful, and for several reasons it will be useful for the following reasons to think of the years 1865 to 1900 as an era in which one American diplomatic paradigm supplanted another:

1. The concept of paradigm change serves as a synthesizer by providing a framework within which we can reconcile interpretations normally considered irreconcilable.

2. The notion of paradigmatic change helps to settle the "discontinuity issue" by explaining some of the domestic and diplomatic shocks America sustained in the late eighties and early nineties, not as mileposts in a gradual slope toward a "new empire" nor as the ups-and-downs expected on a graph of normality, but as "anomalies" creating a favorable climate for men advocating fundamental change.

3. The paradigm idea also helps us make the important point that the new diplomacy of the nineties was more than the sum of its parts. American officials, of course, had to deal with circumstances that had altered gradually over time, but new beliefs and assumptions powerfully affected their view of those conditions. The world described by a chronicler of "facts" might have shifted on its axis only slightly in the twenty years after 1875, but the change sensed by the American diplomatist of 1895 would have been great indeed because of his own transformed perceptions—that is, because of the change in paradigms.

4. In emphasizing not only objectives, but the techniques used to reach them, the paradigm concept supports the view that "imperialism" was not the only, or even the most significant phenomenon of late-nineteenth-century American diplomacy. Important changes simultaneously occurred in the way Americans thought about and conducted foreign policy.

5. Finally, by recognizing that the 1865-89 period, to which the rest of this chapter is devoted, was dominated by a paradigm of its own—instead of seeing it as either an early stage of the "new empire" or a muddled epoch betraying no pattern at all—we can reaffirm its historical integrity. We should resist imposing on it an order that did not exist, or satirizing the period as long done by historians of the Gilded Age. Franz Neumann remarked in *Democratic and Authoritarian States* (1957), that "No greater disservice has ever been rendered political science than the statement that

the liberal state was a 'weak' state. It was precisely as strong as it needed to be in the circumstances.'' Similarly, while avowing that the foreign policy of these years often meandered as erratically as charged, given the terms of the old paradigm this disorder seemed logical enough to Americans at the time.

What to call the two paradigms, which both overlapped and succeeded one another from the end of the eighties to the mid-nineties? Various one-word labels fail to do justice to the characteristics of each paradigm. "Continental" might do for the earlier paradigm were it not for its sole emphasis on location, which ignores the manner and method of American foreign policy. "Imperial" suggests much about the later paradigm, but it gives not a hint of the shift from "incidents" to "policy" noted by Robert Wiebe. Ideally, any acceptable pair of terms should refer to the content, geographical scope, and technique of American foreign policy. But since such precise terms are hard to come by, we will refer simply to the Old and New Paradigms.

How the Old Paradigm gave way to the New and what the latter consisted of in detail are reserved for the next chapter. Here we are concerned with the heyday of the Old Paradigm, extending roughly from the end of the Civil War to the advent of the Harrison administration in 1889. In these years the outlook of American policymakers was generally noninterventionist. Isolationist in spirit, they preferred acting in foreign affairs apart from other nations. Unpracticed in and ambivalent about the use of governmental power, their customary manner of conducting foreign affairs was passive and reactive and involved waiting in Washington for events to happen before responding *ad hoc*; their guidance of diplomats sent abroad, mostly rank amateurs, was minimal and vague. They did not equip their country's army and navy for serious warfare. Complacent congressmen exploited diplomatic issues for partisan ends, just as they did rivers-and-harbors bills and Indian agencies. High state department officials closed shop early, and spent little time defining U.S. "policy." And no wonder, for according to Lord

Bryce's *The American Commonwealth* (1888), the United States still sailed "upon a summer sea." American officials all held to the core assumption of the Old Paradigm: that their nation was safe, her security was threatened nowhere by anyone.

THE *ALABAMA*
CLAIMS AND MEXICO

In 1865 American officials could not avoid dealing with two explosive disputes carried over from the Civil War—one with Great Britain, the other with France. Secretaries of State William H. Seward and Hamilton Fish defused these conflicts with remarkable skill but without the aid of a general policy. They reacted to the problems thrust on them and then sat back to see what would happen next.

The more perilous controversy was with Great Britain. The United States had accused her of illegal, pro-Confederate actions that had injured the Union and prolonged the Civil War. Although England had respected the Union's blockade of Confederate ports, her proclamation of neutrality in May 1861 handed the South the coveted status of belligerent, which included the right to attack Union commerce at sea and send diplomats and bondsellers abroad. Other European governments followed suit with similar declarations. The British subscribed heavily to Richmond's "cotton loan." They looked the other way as Nassau in the Bahamas became a *de facto* Confederate port for blockade-runners. In 1862 Great Britain stopped just short of recognizing Southern independence and proposing mediation of the war, which would have caused war with the United States. In the meantime, British shipyards turned out powerful cruisers for the Confederacy, avoiding technical violation of neutrality laws by a series of flagrant subterfuges. Stern Union protests finally put an end to these sales in 1863, though too late to stop delivery of the *Alabama, Shenan-*

doah, Florida, and other rebel cruisers. These vessels, mostly British-manned, destroyed or disabled about 250 Northern ships, wrecked the Pacific whaling fleet, and boosted maritime insurance rates to prohibitively high levels. More than 700 Yankee merchant ships switched to British registry for self-protection. Unable to act during the war, Seward grimly kept track of the record of damages.

Evidence of a retaliatory spirit appeared as early as 1864, when the United States gave notice (later rescinded) that it would abrogate the Rush-Bagot Treaty and thus free itself to rearm on the Great Lakes. In addition, Congress in 1865 canceled an eleven-year-old reciprocity treaty vital to Canada's prosperity and slapped harsh passport regulations on Canadian travelers. The House passed a neutrality law in 1866 allowing Americans to construct warships for belligerents (raising the specter of future *Alabamas* cruising against British merchant ships) and a year later recorded its hunger for northern territories by protesting the confederation of Canada. Secretary of State Seward dropped hints that cession of British Columbia might satisfy the United States. Actually, the British probably could have settled the *Alabama* claims in 1865 or 1866 with a frank apology. They let the opportunity pass, however, and Americans grew angrier. Just how angry became clear in 1869 when the Senate rejected a settlement hastily put together by the lame-duck Johnson administration. Seeing the Johnson-Clarendon Convention as far too soft on the British, the senators rejected the pact in a stunning 54-1 vote.

Not only had the Senate apparently slammed the door on a moderate settlement, but Charles Sumner of Massachusetts, its greatest luminary in foreign affairs, had dramatically upped the ante in an electrifying speech. British misdeeds, he charged, had caused $15 million in direct damage to American ships—a reasonable figure. But, he added, John Bull was also culpable for "indirect" or "national" damages, such as higher insurance rates, the loss of American merchant ships to British registry ($110 million for these two items), and compensation for goods never risked on the seas for fear of Confederate raids. Most important, he argued that Britain's sly egging on of the rebels doubled the length of the war, the total cost of which he estimated to be $4 billion. "Everybody can make the calculation," he stated, but he also implied that the United States would graciously accept Canada in lieu of cash!

Secretary of State Hamilton Fish inherited the problem just as his old friend Sumner, now a political enemy, was stirring the waters. London remained as unrepentant as ever; Grant, a methodical general but an impulsive president, relished the thought of Phil Sheridan marching into Quebec, or at least scaring the British into turning Canada over to the United States. Vocal Fenians hoped that an Anglo-American war might produce freedom for Ireland. Influential politicians, including the excitable Ben Butler and Nathaniel Banks but also the moderate Carl Schurz (a friend of Sumner), either advocated or tolerated a belligerent policy toward Britain. Few would have blamed the secretary of state had he taken the easy way out, taunting England while the galleries cheered.

But Fish wanted an amicable settlement. His work was cut out for him. Hoping a calmer atmosphere might move events his way, he waited for tempers to cool before resuming formal talks. His first break came when Grant and Sumner clashed over the senator's virulent attack on the project to annex Santo Domingo. Gradually, Fish gained more control over policy, threatening to resign unless Grant gave him a free hand. Businessmen who worried that British capital would abandon U.S. bond markets urged compromise. Republicans, including Grant, began to see in a diplomatic triumph insurance for the president's reelection in 1872. Renewed disputes with Canada over fishing grounds and the San Juan islands boundary in the Northwest reinforced the need for talks. Public attention shifted to other issues. The clincher was probably the realization that most Canadians flatly opposed joining the Union. Fish himself had hoped that jingoistic politicians and an aroused public opinion would force Britain to yield Canada. Instead, he now intimated that the United States would put aside its Canadian ambitions in return for an *Alabama* settlement.

The British also began moving toward a compromise. In 1865 they quietly started withdrawing military units from North America. Victoria's foreign secretary told the queen in 1869 that conflict with the United States "to a great extent paralyses our action in Europe"; continental affairs required full attention and a safe Atlantic flank. Both nations having finally found the will to come to terms, they now decided to go beyond the *Alabama* problem and bring about a general Anglo-American settlement. All outstanding sources of friction were placed on the table, at first in private talks, then in a Joint High Commission hosted by Washington early in 1871. In what became a recurring sequence during the next thirty years, Britain leaned heavily on Canada before she would agree to accords on which diplomats of London and Washington had already shaken hands. The Canadians did come around in May 1871, signing the omnibus Treaty of Washington and joining their fellow negotiators in celebratory strawberries and ice cream. By the terms of the treaty, the San Juan islands boundary dispute was submitted to German arbitration and later settled in favor of the United States. American fishing rights in Canadian waters were expanded in exchange for a *quid pro quo* in American waters for British subjects plus a cash award of $5.5 million (settled on in 1877) to Canada. The St. Lawrence River was permanently opened to U.S. shipping in return for opening three major rivers in Alaska to Canadian vessels.

On the *Alabama* claims, Great Britain expressed her regret for the actions of the Confederate cruisers without "apologizing" or admitting to illegal acts. The Washington Treaty provided for damage figures to be set by an arbitration tribunal in Geneva made up of representatives from Brazil, Italy, Switzerland, and the two contesting parties; in making its decision the tribunal was instructed to use standards of neutral conduct that guaranteed an award acceptable to the United States. The treaty said nothing about "indirect" claims, an issue the British confidently thought they had heard the last of. But Hamilton Fish had an opportunistic side, too. Despite what he had apparently told British negotiators in Washington, he ordered the issue reopened in Geneva. His motives were probably twofold, first to win partisan points by catering to jingoes at home and—shrewdly if still unstatesmanlike—to get the issue settled definitively in international law. As Adrian Cook remarks, "it is not easy to justify his reputation as a great secretary of state upon his conduct of the Alabama Claims negotiations." The outraged British stormed over what looked like a Yankee trick. Nor, with the Franco-Prussian War ended and the most recent dispute over the Black Sea resolved, were they so desperate for accord as formerly. The whole agreement nearly came unglued. But Charles Francis Adams, scion of presidents and the American member of the Geneva tribunal, dreamed up a face-saving formula for all parties: the arbitrators announced that they had taken solemn notice of the indirect claims (placating the Americans) but had not found them deserving of official consideration (mollifying the British). The five-man body then completed its work in September 1872 with a $15.5 million award to the United States for direct damages. The process of patient discussion and compromise known as "diplomacy" had settled a dangerous conflict, and bows were in order to everyone involved, even the inconstant Hamilton Fish.

The second important problem left over from the Civil War, though neither so dangerous nor resistant to settlement, was the French establishment of a Hapsburg puppet, Ferdinand Maximilian, as emperor of Mexico. The story began in 1861, when France, Britain, and Spain sent a joint military expedition to collect debts repudiated by the Mexican Congress. The United States had warily rejected an invitation to join what was purportedly a routine debt-collecting enterprise. Britain and Spain, though the latter was sympathetic, withdrew from the venture after realizing that Napoleon III intended to create in the New World a Catholic monarchy beholden to French power. Napoleon, hoping to gratify Catholics and confound critics by strutting on the world stage, believed he could set a brake on the growth of American power. Despite tenacious resistance from President Benito Juárez and the forces of the Mexican Republic, Napoleon and 110,000 French troops gained effective control of the country by 1864. Maximilian and his ambitious empress Carlota sat somewhat uneasily on the ancient throne of Montezuma.

Preoccupied by the Union military defeats of 1861-62, Seward politely registered American displeasure and bided his time, though he feared that Juárez might look for help from a Confederacy bearing blandishments. As both the North's victories and Napoleon's troubles at home mounted, however, the secretary of state began turning the screw. The United States refused to break off diplomatic relations with Juárez's guerrilla regime and stepped up the pace of its complaints to Paris. In 1864 the House of Representatives advertised its impatience by unanimously demanding French withdrawal. Finally, with the Civil War at an end, 50,000 battle-tested bluecoats led by General Sheridan stood poised on the Mexican border, ordered to observe strict neutrality but tacitly permitted to harass Maximilian's forces while offering aid and comfort to the loyalists. The mouse might play while the cat was away, but now the cat was back.

If President Andrew Johnson had followed General Grant's demand for "decisive measures," the rough stuff could have started right away. The more cautious Seward adroitly mapped his own course. As Gordon H. Warren has written, his approach was "firmness in public, conciliation in private." Seward warned France that an aroused public might overcome his own temperate preferences, urged Napoleon to remove his troops, and graciously held the door for their departure. Believing that without French support Maximilian would topple of his own weight, Seward refrained from demanding the dismantlement of the puppet empire; nor, despite pressure to do so, did he wave the Monroe Doctrine in Napoleon's face. He insisted only that French troops leave Mexico. At first France offered withdrawal if the United States would recognize Maximilian; Seward responded by sending a new minister to Juárez's regime. Napoleon saw the game was up when Britain turned down his bid for help and when Seward on February 12, 1866, told Paris that he must receive a specific date of withdrawal. Napoleon's adventure had grown noxious at home, and his troops were needed for European contingencies. In April 1866 France announced it would soon withdraw; the last soldier left a year later. The Empire collapsed, and Maximilian was captured and executed after scorning chances to escape. One of many tragedies for the Hapsburg family, for the United States the Mexican affair was a signal victory in the struggle for power in the Western Hemisphere.

SEWARD, GRANT, AND BLAINE

Seward and Fish adhered to no general "policy" in the *Alabama* and Mexico affairs; instead they reacted to incidents as they arose. A few historians have contended, however, that a purposeful drive toward empire emerged immediately after the Civil War—that what I am calling the New Paradigm arrived on the scene long before the nineties. Prominently identified with this alleged epoch of deliberate and expansionist policymaking are Seward's post–Civil War years as secretary of state (1865–69), the Grant-Fish period (1869–77), and James G. Blaine's first term as secretary of state (1881). This argument requires attention before going on to describe and note the character of other important developments in the era.

Seward's case is the most intriguing because, over three decades, he periodically announced his adherence to an elaborate imperial design. According to this bold-spirited

New Yorker, the course of history, the dictates of Providence, the logic of commerce, and the necessities of military strategy all pointed to the growth of a great and peacefully-acquired American empire. For centuries the locus of the world's great empires had been moving westward; now America, in God's eye, stood on center stage; to enjoy continued industrial progress and security from Old World aggression, it must follow the course plotted for it to Asia and the Pacific—after laying down the necessary foundation. Seward prescribed high tariffs and cheap labor to accelerate industrialization, rapid settlement of the West, and an efficient rail and canal network that would bring together resources, markets, and peoples in a combination of economic power and political unity.

But his vision did not dictate a specific program. Seward's expansionism, in the view of Adrian Cook and others, had its source in a politician's desire for public acclaim, an intellectual's yen for historical reputation, and a craving personality's undifferentiated need for power. The author of flatulent rhetoric on any subject, he often sounded like nothing more than a Davey Crockett spread-eagle; he declared in 1867 that, with continued peace at home and "fifty, forty, and thirty more years of life," he could give the United States "the possession of the American continent and the control of the world." Charles Francis Adams confided to his diary in 1867 that "Mr. Seward's thirst for more land seems insatiable," suggesting that a haphazard hunger for glory lay behind the belief in a future American Empire stretching from the Arctic Circle to Panama (with its capital in Mexico City). Something like greed rather than diplomatic planning nourished his hopes, expressed at various times, of attaching to the Union not only Alaska and Midway, but Santo Domingo, Haiti, Martinique, the Virgin Islands, the Bahamas, Cuba, Puerto Rico, St. Bartholomew's Island, Tiger Island (off the west coast of Central America), St. Pierre and Miquelon in the St. Lawrence, Iceland, Greenland, British Columbia, Hawaii, and, if rumors could be credited, Fiji and Borneo. Resembling Theodore Roosevelt's bi-ennial itch for a war, Seward's pulsating imperialism was probably aimed more at shoring up the Johnson administration and his own chances for the presidency than at achieving well-defined policy goals.

shallow goals

Seward's record was notable, nonetheless, quite apart from his skillful handling of Civil War diplomacy and the Mexican affair. Besides acquiring Alaska and backing the navy's occupation of Midway Island in 1867, he joined European powers in defending Western treaty rights in Japan and China, strove to tighten commercial links with Hawaii, and opened the American West to thousands of Chinese laborers in the 1868 Burlingame treaty. He was forever dickering for Caribbean naval bases (though the crumbling U.S. fleet needed new bases far less than wholesale repair), but the only deal he could nail down was an agreement to purchase the Danish West Indies (Virgin Islands). The stories of Alaska and the Virgin Islands, in particular, deserve fuller discussion.

Luck

The purchase of Alaska achieved one of Seward's goals—the extension of American power to the north Pacific—but he fell on this *coup* as luckily as Jefferson did Louisiana. Russians for years had considered dumping Alaska because of its high cost to the state, vulnerability to British seizure, and, as Howard I. Kushner has shown, the pressure brought on the territory by enterprising Americans worming their way into every cranny of its economy. St. Petersburg had broached a sale to the United States in 1854 and returned to the subject in 1860. Talks secretly resumed in March 1867. Concluded rapidly in an all-night session (after the Russian minister got the go-ahead from the czar over the new transatlantic cable), the treaty gave Alaska to the United States for $7.2 million, or 2 cents an acre. As every schoolchild knows, some Americans mocked the purchase as "Seward's Icebox," or condemned the treaty as "a dark deed done in the night," but many newspapers rallied to the treaty's support. Senators quickly approved, 37 to 2, not only because Seward entertained them with "toothsome dinners, meats, and drinks," as Paul S. Holbo has written, but also because Seward and their colleague Charles Sumner convincingly demonstrated Alaska's economic and strategic value.

Another reason for the Senate's favorable vote was its eagerness to please Russia, America's good "friend"—and therein lies a story. Americans had long enjoyed regarding Russia as friendly. This wishful thinking was reinforced in 1863 when Russian fleets paid ostentatiously amicable calls at the ports of New York and San Francisco. Excited Northerners, smarting from Europe's hostility to the Union, viewed the visits as a show of Russian support and responded with an emotional outburst of gratitude. A half century after the parades, banquets, and champagne toasts to bemused czarist naval captains had ended, scholarship caught up with Russia's real purposes: she had dispatched her Baltic and Asiatic fleets to America to keep them from being bottled up in their home ports should a war ensue with Britain over the Polish revolt. Lincoln and Seward grasped Russia's unsentimental object but did not let on, hoping the visits would give pause to pro-Confederate groups in London and Paris. Oblivious of the power politics involved, however, most Americans were still awash in the friendship myth in 1867. Only a year earlier, when Czar Alexander II barely escaped an attempt on his life, Congress declared its gratitude to "the nation that had given us its warmest sympathies in our hour of peril." The Senate would probably have consented in any case, but approving Seward's treaty to avoid offending Russia was a popular cry; Charles Sumner, though he knew better, declared that the fleet visit of 1863 was "a friendly demonstration" ordered by the czar. Yet despite quick Senate approval, tight-fisted House members delayed voting the purchase money until July 1868, when the appropriation finally carried amid gossip that the Russian minister had bought the necessary votes.

In 1867, many saw Alaska as the upper jaw of a vise

tightened on British Columbia; the great strategic value of Seward's bargain remained unclear until the beginning of the Cold War with a Russia no longer ruled by czars. Meanwhile, Seward carried on a lonely search for Caribbean naval bases. The navy department was unenthusiastic. Congress foiled attempts to institute protectorates in Haiti and Santo Domingo or annex the island of Hispaniola cohabited by these two republics. Success seemed near in October 1867 when Seward arranged the purchase of St. Thomas and St. John in the Danish West Indies, fearing that Prussia or Austria might otherwise get them. A plebiscite in the islands endorsed the change before Denmark ratified the pact in January 1868, but at the last moment Congress balked. The price tag of $7.5 million seemed particularly high in light of the hurricane and tidal wave that beached the USS *Monongahela* on St. Thomas almost before the signatures on the treaty had dried. Nor did an earthquake on nearby St. Croix seem persuasive. Efforts to revive the agreement persisted as late as 1870, but to no avail; the Wilson administration completed Seward's project in 1917.

If Seward's imperialism had a buckshot quality to it, it was a model of deliberateness compared with Grant's. Most of President Grant's expansionist moves, Marilyn B. Young observes, are best understood "in terms of his total administration, whose dominant characteristic was one of grab." Even Grant's grabbiness was erratic. He once shrugged off a suggestion to annex French Guiana, apparently from a sensible lack of interest, but he also allowed Seward's barely breathing Virgin Islands treaty to languish because he disliked its author. So much for the power of reason in foreign policy!

However helter-skelter the course, the Grant administration kept up the trend toward expansionism. Secretary of State Hamilton Fish pushed hard for protection of U.S. rights in China. In 1875 officials made a reciprocal trade agreement with Hawaii that tied its economy tightly to the mainland and forbade the sale of any Hawaiian territory to other nations. Following a treaty concluded during the Johnson administration that secured nonexclusive transit rights through Nicaragua, Grant's diplomats arrived at a similar pact with Colombia for U.S. rights across Panama. The Senate ignored this agreement, but the president appointed a special canal commission that eventually recommended digging any canal along the Nicaraguan route. By declaring in 1870 "that hereafter no territory on this continent shall be regarded as subject to transfer to a European power," Grant also linked the so-called No Transfer principle to the Monroe Doctrine. An isolated statement of curiosity to chroniclers of the Monroe Doctrine, it had no other significance.

In his most significant reach into the Caribbean, Grant aimed at annexing Santo Domingo (today's Dominican Republic). Why did he want Santo Domingo? "Grab" for one reason, glory and power for others. If pressed for concrete reasons to annex this troubled republic, he might have listed several: Santo Domingo, he thought, would give the United States a valuable naval base, boost the business community, supply a new home for ex-slaves, and perhaps provide a sanitarium site for future canal workers struck down by tropical fevers. Besides, the ever impenitent, impecunious, and importunate Dominican rulers had once again put their country up for auction, and Grant never found an attractive deal easy to pass up. Acting without advice, he sent General Orville Babcock, one of his less savory aides, to make the contract; Babcock returned with a treaty giving the United States options of annexing Santo Domingo or leasing Samaná Bay. After renegotiation late in 1869 (for Babcock had been unauthorized to sign a treaty) the pact called for puchasing Santo Domingo for $1.5 million, in which case the new territory could aspire to eventual statehood, or renting Samaná Bay for $150,000 a year with a first option to buy.

As the Senate mulled over the treaty, seven U.S. warships patrolled Dominican waters with orders to "destroy or capture" Haitian ships if they attacked the territory. Grant personally twisted senators' arms in Capitol hallways and deferentially called at the home of Charles Sumner, departing with what he took to be a promise of support. But the Senate grandee assaulted the treaty instead, as did many other Republicans, stopping ratification ten votes short of approval in June 1870. Secretary of State Fish had stood by the treaty out of loyalty to the president and because the obsession with Santo Domingo kept Grant out of his hair in dealing with the *Alabama* claims and Cuba (see below). Grant tried several times to resuscitate the project but was unsuccessful, even after having the apostate Sumner purged as chairman of the Senate Committee on Foreign Relations.

Not only senators opposed the Dominican treaty. Leading opinion makers across the nation fought the project, using arguments that foreshadowed the anti-imperialist campaign of 1898–1900. Ernest R. May contends that this wave of anti-imperialism was influenced by a contemporaneous disdain for colonialism in Europe, but Old World views aside, opponents in the United States responded to old values and prejudices alike. They protested the cost of expansionist projects and feared the mischief-making potential of new naval bases. Except for advanced liberals such as Sumner, they believed Reconstruction had shown the folly of incorporating "alien" races within the political system and worried about absorbing the "semi-savage" Catholics of Santo Domingo. Most of all, they condemned Grant's scheme for crossing the barrier that American traditions had erected against the "European" practice of imperialism.

Anti-imperialists also looked with jaundiced concern on Cuba, where a civil war destined to last a decade broke out in 1868. By the time Grant was inaugurated, the war had descended to savagery. American citizens were being killed and U.S. property destroyed. From their sanctuary in the United States, Cuban rebel groups were attracting cash and sympathy from American supporters. Public opinion began turning sharply against Spain.

Americans had taken a proprietary interest in Cuba for

three-quarters of a century and more than once intrigued for its cession to the United States. The last major European possession to the south, Cuba sparkled with temptation for those with eyes for her economic potential and strategic location. Early in 1869, Grant's busybody impulses and Congress's excited interest made American intervention appear likely. These conditions seemed to promise war with Spain and annexation of the island (an idea Cuban rebels whispered into the ears of U.S. officials). As a token of Grant's interest, ships of the Pacific squadron made their way to the West Indies to reinforce a sizable flotilla already patrolling the Cuban vicinity.

The greatest obstacle to intervention may have been Hamilton Fish, who hoped to persuade Spain to assuage the rebels through internal reform. He was determined to prevent the Cuban affair from obstructing an *Alabama* settlement and to keep Congress from following half a dozen Latin American nations in recognizing the rebels' belligerency. Fish opposed such a step for several reasons. He thought the rebels' accomplishments did not warrant the status of belligerency. Taking such an action might also harm the U.S. case against British recognition of Southern belligerency in 1861. Moreover, Spain bore financial responsibility for damages to U.S. property only as long as Washington stuck to the status quo. Fish may have had nightmares of radical seizures of that property if the rebellion succeeded. Having a son-in-law representing Spain's legal interests in New York may even have influenced him.

But most important, such a forward move would probably cause war, not a prospect Fish relished. A war with Spain, he felt, would be harder to win than armchair patriots thought. Besides, it would magnify the national debt, aggravate sores on the body politic, and lead inexorably to the annexation of Cuba. Although Fish made clear that the United States would not tolerate annexation by any other nation, he did not want Cuba for the United States. A Hudson River patrician, he sniffed at the pretensions of the Cubans, utterly unqualified in his view for the American Union's blessings. But because he was convinced that Spain could never end the rebellion with arms, he repeatedly pressed Madrid to pull up the roots of dissension through reform, including the abolition of slavery.

He eventually achieved some success through luck and his own dexterity. From the start, Fish had to stave off effusions such as the House resolution of April 10, 1869, which expressed sympathy for the rebellion and assured support for Grant if he recognized a state of belligerency. Hoping to preempt more drastic action, Fish boldly approached Spain that summer and urged Madrid first to call a cease-fire and abolish slavery, then allow the Cubans to buy their freedom for about $100 million, the payment to be guaranteed by the United States. While Spain played for time, Grant suddenly asked the flabbergasted Fish to issue an already prepared proclamation recognizing Cuban belligerency after notarizing it with the state department seal. Fish for the moment pigeonholed the document; and Grant, by then totally absorbed with Santo Domingo, unaccountably forgot all about it! In the spring of 1870 Fish felt compelled to stage a showdown. With another belligerency resolution about to emerge from the House and Grant again rustling combatively, the secretary of state threatened to resign unless the president halted his interference in routine state department business and publicly dissociated himself from the jingoes. The victor of Appomattox retreated. Fish took unchallenged control of Cuban policy. The House, told by Grant to stifle its offending resolution, voted it down 101-88 on June 16, 1870.

Although Spain did not respond positively to the ambitious American démarche of 1869, Cuba returned to the diplomatic backburner until 1873, when a sudden crisis nearly destroyed Fish's hopes for peace. In October, a Spanish warship seized a rebel-owned vessel, the *Virginius,* in international waters. Laden with arms and falsely flying the Stars and Stripes, the ship was hauled to a Cuban port. There, after kangaroo-court trials, a firing squad executed fifty-three of the *Virginius's* passengers and crewmen, including some U.S. citizens. More would have died except for a forceful British intervention. Fish could barely contain the public uproar, but passions subsided after the ship's fraudulent American registry was revealed. London pressed Spain to settle, and once Fish shifted the talks from the Spanish capital to Washington, finessing the umbrageous American minister Dan Sickles, Madrid agreed to an $80,000 indemnity for the families of U.S. citizens who had been executed.

After the crisis, Fish wrote that "Spain must soon admit the fact that the Island has fallen from her control." In 1875 he tried once again to find a solution to Cuba's agony, but the rebels were already losing strength and neither Spain nor other European powers would go along. Nor were the American people still interested, for the chances of a conflict with Spain over Cuba had faded rapidly after the *Virginius* affair.

Here it is worthwhile to compare the peaceful conclusion of the 1873 crisis and the descent to war in 1898. At least six important differences distinguish the two cases. (1) War seemed far less acceptable during the deep autumn depression of 1873 than in the prosperous spring of 1898. (2) In 1873 many Americans sympathized with the Spanish government, then briefly under republican rule, and realized that those responsible for the worst outrages in Cuba were hard-liners beyond Madrid's control. No such sympathy existed in 1898. (3) Few Americans doubted the phony status of the *Virginius* but almost all thought in 1898 that Spanish treachery had destroyed the *Maine*. (4) Spain appeared eager to make amends in 1873 but intransigent twenty-five years later. (5) U.S. public opinion, only fitfully aroused by foreign alarms in the 1870s, had entered an advanced state of jingoism by 1898. (6) Not only was Fish opposed to war but was aware that available to him were a 30,000-man army pronounced "entirely inadequate" by General William T. Sherman and a navy an officer later recalled as capable of nothing but "making faces at the Spaniards." Those in power in 1898 dealt from a stronger military base and in some cases lusted for combat.

The civil war in Cuba ended in 1878, and slavery was soon abolished, but another round of violence was only a matter of time. As the years passed, U.S. economic influence grew larger. Even while civil war raged in the seventies, American trade with Cuba came to exceed U.S. commerce with all other Latin American nations combined. With an eye for wartime opportunity, American investors bought out many strapped local landowners. Hamilton Fish had held the United States out of the war and indirectly helped his countrymen penetrate the Cuban economy. His intermittent support of Cuban independence also departed from both John Quincy Adams's policy of tolerating Spanish rule until time ripened for a U.S. takeover and the eager antebellum push for annexation. The significance of these changes, however, is easily exaggerated; the United States did not so much have a Cuban policy as a Fish policy, which could be altered 180 degrees in a twinkling. Genuine continuity on Cuban matters still awaited a new paradigm of diplomacy itself.

During James G. Blaine's nine months as secretary of state in 1881, he invited eighteen Western Hemisphere republics to attend an inter-American conference in Washington. The meeting was canceled after he resigned late in the year, though it was revived and chaired by Blaine himself in 1889-90 during a second tour at the state department. Though his project was aborted in 1881, markets-minded historians construe his role in laying the cornerstone of pan-Americanism as a farsighted attempt to promote peaceful settlement of hemispheric disputes and, especially, to create the instruments of export expansionism in Latin America.

Blaine did worry about the many wars between Latin states, and he was troubled by the poor trading record of the United States in hemisphere markets, but he probably worried even more about European political influence in the area. The issues were closely related. A hemisphere at peace would generally stimulate trade; closer bonds with nations to the south would open doors for American goods; and peace combined with a better U.S. trade performance would diminish European influence. Thus reconstructed, Blaine's reasoning seems impressively logical, but his 1881 pan-Americanism probably grew from more egoistic seeds. Blaine's diplomatic background was nil; never before 1881 had he spoken about an inter-American conference. He had long been known, however, as an inveterate activist, and his ambition to be both President Garfield's "prime minister" and his successor was common currency. From what became known as a "spirited" foreign policy, he expected direct, personal advantage. An intelligent man, Blaine at a glance could see tempting issues dotted across the hemisphere, a perfect arena for a display of "spirit." The "Plumed Knight" grasped his lance and began thrusting—with alarming results.

First he charged into a boundary dispute between Mexico and Guatemala, asking Mexico to accept impartial arbitration while all too obviously taking Guatemala's side himself. Mexico first demurred politely enough but, when Blaine persisted, testily rejected the proposal. The fray over the boundary dragged on in spite of Blaine, who had managed only to offend an important neighbor. Farther south, where Costa Rica and Colombia had agreed to a European nation's arbitration in another border fracas, Blaine chimed in with loud cries against old world intrusions in the hemisphere, again accomplishing nothing but the lowering of U.S. stock in Latin America.

Then Blaine ensnared himself in the War of the Pacific, which since 1879 had pitted Chile against Peru and Bolivia in a struggle to control coastal areas rich in nitrates and guano. Chile had won the military contest handily but could not wrap up the peace because Peru, particularly, refused to accept Chile's large territorial gains. The United States had already tried mediating the impasse without success, but Blaine was eager to give it another try. Counting on political

capital for himself in any diplomatic victory, he wanted the
United States to take a stand against armed expansion in the
hemisphere. He also hoped to cut pro-British Chile down to
size and aid Peru before it looked to Europe for help.
Throughout, as Joseph Smith has shown, he grossly exaggerated British efforts to influence the region, which twisted
his views into a spiral of anti-Chilean prejudice. Thus, in yet
another biased intervention that could only go wrong,
Blaine, as Smith writes, "incurred a reputation for aggressive and reckless diplomacy. . . ." While Chile bristled with
anger, Blaine's personal choices for ministers guaranteed
further ridicule for himself: Hugh Judson Kilpatrick took
Chile's side in Santiago, Stephen Hurlbut trumpeted Peru's
in Lima, and the two men publicly paraded their disagree-
ment in the newspapers (a "display of pretentious in-
capacity," wrote Britain's minister to Peru). As one historian has remarked, his ministers were "ill-paid, ill-trained,
and ill-tempered," but here it was Blaine who failed to control them or even to answer all their dispatches.

Belatedly aware of this mess, Blaine looked desperately
for a way to rescue his "spirited" foreign policy. First he
sent a special agent to South America to reimpose a united
front on his own representatives and to persuade Brazil and
Argentina to back the U.S. position. He then got President
Chester A. Arthur, who had just succeeded the murdered
Garfield, to send conference invitations to all the Latin
American states except black-ruled Haiti. What Blaine had
in mind, according to persuasive articles published thirty
years ago by Russell H. Bastert, was threefold: to recoup his
political fortunes; to restore a facade of success to the
shambles of his policy through a showy gesture; and to use
other states' presence at an inter-American conference to
force Mexico into line on its dispute with Guatemala, and
Chile into returning some of its loot from the War of the
Pacific. The invitations said nothing about commercial issues; nor did Blaine ever connect the subject with the con-

ference until responding to attacks on his record after leaving office. Charles S. Campbell argues that Blaine's policies were aimed at "potential" rather than "existing" interests. Perhaps his manifold problems can therefore be partly attributed to his anticipation of future issues. Nonetheless, his 1881 "policies" can best be understood as a hodgepodge of political opportunism, hasty patchwork, and misdirected energy.

Blaine's successor, Frederick T. Frelinghuysen, certainly did not think he was damaging an important "policy" when he withdrew the conference invitations. On the contrary, information on his hands indicated that both Mexico and Chile, as well as several European nations, were deeply suspicious of the scheduled gathering. Other sources suggested that friends of Blaine stood to profit financially from an anti-Chilean settlement of the War of the Pacific. Although American good offices eventually helped bring this war to an end, Washington reaped no goodwill as a result. Few mediators ever have.

A NAVY FIT ENOUGH

In Oscar Wilde's *Canterville Ghost*, the English wraith and American maiden discuss the new world:

"I don't think I should like America."

"I suppose because we have no ruins and no curiosities," said Virginia sarcastically.

"No ruins! No curiosities!" answered the Ghost; "you have your navy and your manners."

Historians have found the Gilded Age U.S. Navy as tempting to satirize as the diplomatic corps. It seemed to many fit only for firewood. Alfred T. Mahan recalled the visit of a French officer to an American man-of-war; the Frenchman pointed to the guns, sighed nostalgically, and remarked: *"Ah! Capitaine, les vieux canons!"* Mahan himself said in

1882: "We have not six ships that would be kept at sea by any maritime power."

But this navy conformed to American needs as defined by the Old Paradigm. Lance C. Buhl argues that, given what national policymakers of the era sought and expected, "The United States Navy, both conceptually and operationally, was a perfectly viable and adequate arm of the national government in the twenty-five years following the Civil War."

The large Union navy did not immediately diminish after 1865, Washington making sure that France withdrew from Mexico as scheduled. But deep budget cuts began in 1867. Wooden ships *were* converted to firewood; ironclads rusted in dry dock; new technology in armament and propulsion arose unnoticed. But since this decay occurred at a time officials could sense no external danger to the nation, navy men found little to protest in their service's deterioration. They settled into a comfortable, if monotonous duty, their ships, George Dewey remembered, only going "from port to port to meet . . . wives . . . and to get letters from sweethearts." This was a navy that avoided rough waters, sticking to routine duties in the Caribbean, Mediterranean, and the Pacific. It showed the flag and guarded missionaries against heathen outrages, but it gave a wide berth to truly great navies. (The same held true in the army. Since, as James Abrahamson writes, officers neither expected a foreign attack on the United States nor vice versa, their army in the 1870s and 1880s was "ill-equipped, weakened by decentralization . . . , irrationally administered," and unsure of its role. With no planning board, the U.S. Army had "no choice but to respond to any new crisis in an ad hoc fashion, substituting improvisation for careful analysis and purposeful preparation." None of this, however, seemed as awful to contemporary officers as to later observers.)

However safe the country, by the end of the seventies its naval officers saw the need for some kind of revival. Naval reform started under Secretary of the Navy William E. Chandler in the Arthur administration (1881-85). Historians have usually viewed the later building program, under President Harrison and his secretary Benjamin F. Tracy (1889-93), as an accelerated, more ambitious extension of the Arthur-Chandler program. But these two reform navies belonged to distinct eras, however near to one another by the calendar. Chandler's officers and contractors built ships designed for cruising and defense in an age of security; Tracy's laid the keels for a great navy that would carry the fight to the fleets of dangerous enemies.

Still an organization of autonomous baronies, the squadrons of the eighties operated independently of one another. "No general staff," Abrahamson writes, "studied the future or ensured that the bureaus worked in harmony as they prepared the navy to meet it." Chandler founded both the Naval War College and Office of Naval Intelligence but assigned them traditional tasks; he reduced an inflated officer corps. His goals were efficiency and professionalism, his approach evolutionary. The navy he created remained small—outranked as late as 1884 by no fewer than eleven other navies. It was also, notes James A. Field, Jr., still "purely defensive, intended only 'as a police force for the preservation of order and never for aggression. . . .' " It was still led by doctrinal conservatives reluctant to surrender sail for steam. It was still starved by a Congress that, through the eighties, never spent more than 1 percent of the gross national product on the military. Congressmen, who flatly refused a request for a 17 percent increase in personnel during the *Virginius* crisis, were not simply stingy. They and their successors of the eighties knew what they were doing, Buhl writes, and saw "absolutely no reason to compete with European nations. The integrity of the hemisphere, despite two early crises with France and Spain, was not at stake; nor could any conceivable interest be served by addition of territory across the seas."

This sense of security was temporary, however. As the eighties drew to a close, a few men freshly sensitive to external dangers chafed at a navy they now saw as powerless to deter potential enemies. How could the U.S. show its seriousness in Samoa with a navy routinely incapable of stationing modern ships in the southwest Pacific? What once seemed normal would soon appear intolerable, as one diplomatic paradigm succeeded another—William Chandler's navy disappeared in the wake of Benjamin Tracy's.

Succession

DAY-TO-DAY DIPLOMATIC PREOCCUPATIONS

But that time had not yet come. In the sixties, seventies, and eighties, American officials acted impulsively more than consistently. They often showed less concern for the national interest than for their own political interests. Their day-to-day preoccupations revolved around humdrum events usually ignored by historians (Milton Plesur's *America's Outward Thrust: Approaches to Foreign Affairs, 1865-1890* [1971] is a welcome exception). They lavished energy on protecting American citizens who had gotten into trouble abroad, especially naturalized citizens: Irish-Americans meddling in the movement for a free Ireland, Jews harassed on innocent visits to relatives in Russia or pilgrimages in Palestine, among others. Most trouble-prone of all were Christian missionaries, especially in Asia and the Mideast. According to one estimate, in the late nineteenth century officers in the Constantinople legation spent nine-tenths of their time toiling over missionary issues. As much as their counterparts in the navy, these soul savers in faraway fields often took initiatives that compelled Washington to react with short-term ("policies.)" Another time-consuming, uncelebrated issue was the border friction caused by Mexican bandits and horse thieves, which led to nearly twenty punitive raids by U.S. troopers in the seventies and eighties. In time these fracases along the Rio Grande gave way to a traffic of American investors going south with money for the mines, railroads, and petroleum of Mexico. But while they lasted, border troubles had monopolized many an official's time in both Washington and Mexico City.

Most of the issues facing American officials in the *CANAL* 1865-89 period arose nearby. The hardiest perennial was the interoceanic canal. Since the United States had several times failed to gain a canal site via treaty, Washington was concerned by the 1879 announcement that Ferdinand de Lesseps of Suez Canal fame would head a French firm intending to build a canal through Panama. Both the Senate and House passed critical resolutions; after a leisurely pause, President Hayes declared on March 8, 1880, that the United States could not tolerate a canal controlled by "any European power [de Lesseps, however, represented a private firm, not a government] or . . . combination of European powers," adding for good measure that any canal "would be . . . virtually a part of the coast line of the United States." De Lesseps, whose company dug itself into bankruptcy within ten years, was only one of Washington's problems. How to undo the Clayton-Bulwer Treaty was another. Signed in 1850, this pact banned Britain (and the United States) from colonizing any part of Central America, but it also forbade Washington from building or operating a canal except as a joint venture with London. Attempts to untie this obnoxious knot climaxed in Secretary of State Frelinghuysen's remarkable Nicaraguan treaty of 1884, in which he gained a route across Central America, but only by claiming that the 1850 treaty had "lapsed by neglect"! The Senate, squirming at this blatant pretext and leery of terms that obliged the United States to protect Nicaragua's sovereignty, sighed with regret and defeated the agreement. A motion to reconsider gave new hope to supporters, but President Cleveland withdrew the treaty from the Senate shortly after entering office in 1885. There the matter stood for fifteen years. (At the same time in what Cleveland regarded as an unrelated incident, he sent the marines to restore order in Panama during a brief revolt against Colombia's central government, acting on authority provided in the 1846 New Granada treaty.)

A constant problem for the United States was Canada, the source of almost every point of conflict still outstanding between the United States and Great Britain. Problems arose in the 1860s because of Fenian raids into Canadian territory, calculated to free Ireland in a British-American war. But the most vexatious conflicts centered on American rights in Canadian fishing grounds. Questions of cod had so relentlessly plagued U.S.-British relations, one might imagine the Founding Fathers concluding their labors in 1787 with a special injunction that, "It shall be the duty of the Executive, Congress, and People alike to argue in perpetuity with Great Britain over the fisheries of His Britannic Majesty's Dominions of North America." This boring argument, which began even before 1787, had supposedly been stifled in the 1871 Treaty of Washington. But the settlement broke down; it was patched again; and finally it collapsed in 1886. Canada seized American violators and fined them. Congress retorted by empowering the president to keep all Canadian goods and ships out of American waters. Cleveland used these powers in 1888 as a "bargaining chip" in securing a new agreement, which was rejected by a Republican Senate. While Cleveland and Congress wrangled to no purpose, diplomats quietly worked out a two-year *modus vivendi*. Periodically renewed, it remained the "law" on Canadian fisheries issues until 1898–99, when another attempt was made at a permanent settlement that ended in equal futility.

In 1886 a dispute broke out in the Bering Sea when the United States cracked down on Canadians engaged in pelagic sealing (hunting seals in the open seas). In Samuel F. Bemis's notorious description, "Amphibious is the fur seal, ubiquitous and carnivorous, uniparous, gregarious and withal polygamous." Their home was the American Pribilof Islands, where hunters killed thousands annually within quotas designed to preserve the herd. Unregulated pelagic sealing, which took a high toll in females, endangered the herd's life and jeopardized a valued American business. U.S. seizures of Canadian ships on the high seas in 1886–87 provoked angry protests in Ottawa and London, whereupon Congress proclaimed the affected waters a closed sea (*mare clausum*), under domestic jurisdiction. When new seizures began in 1889, Britain moved warships in position to defend Canadian sealers. The diplomatic logjam began breaking after American hunting was revealed to threaten the seal herd as much as pelagic sealing. First a temporary arrangement calmed crisis nerves, then the disputants agreed to international arbitration. In 1893 arbitrators meeting in Paris ruled flatly against the United States on the *mare clausum* question, ordered damages paid to the Canadians, and restricted future U.S. rights to a traditional three miles off the shores of the seal islands. To Washington's relief, the arbitrators also acted to protect the herd by closing a zone within sixty miles of the islands to all pelagic fishing and forbidding pelagic sealing elsewhere for three months of each year. With this settlement, the trend toward better U.S.–British relations continued despite Fenians, fish, and fur seals.

U.S. involvement in Europe remained minimal. Almost the only issue to disturb American ties to the continent resulted from restrictions placed in the 1880s by France and Germany on American meat imports, particularly pork. Although official complaints of tainted meat were partially legitimate, the heart of the "pork wars" was a European effort to protect its livestock growers from American competitors. After Washington threatened to embargo all imports from countries discriminating against U.S. products and to hamstring the sale of German sugar in the United States, the disputes were resolved in 1890–91. To the south and east, the tottering Ottoman Empire attracted big-power concentration, which accelerated a post-Civil War decline of U.S. influence in the area. A modest presence established by a few missionaries, merchants, educators, naval officers, and diplomats in Greece, Turkey, Bulgaria, and Egypt, virtually disappeared. These Americans had merely dabbled where the Russians and British played for keeps. Thus, when Washington discovered during the Bulgarian massacres of the 1870s that low-level American diplomats were marginally involved in explosive issues, it summarily reined them in.

America's chronic lack of interest in Africa changed little, even after Captain Robert Shufeldt in a great voyage of the late 1870s gained U.S. rights to a coaling station in Madagascar, signed a trade pact with the Sultan of Johanna in the Comoro Islands, visited Zanzibar and the Persian Gulf, and urged his government to encourage trade along the western coast of Africa. Washington murmured approvingly, but no action followed. The United States now and then displayed a special solicitude for Liberia's welfare, but no European challenge ever put the claim to test. Henry S. Sanford demonstrated how a clever private citizen could seize the machinery of a weak central government in the era of the Old Paradigm by convincing the Arthur administration in 1884 to attend the Berlin West African Conference. Hoping to protect the open door in the Congo, Sanford and the other U.S. delegates signed the Berlin Treaty after doing much to gain their goals. The president approved their work but was soon out of office. The incoming Cleveland, a specialist in spurning the handiwork of predecessors, thought the treaty dangerously entangling and buried it.

In Asia and the Pacific, the United States followed an assertive, sometimes adventurous course resulting in a sharp increase of activity in China, Japan, Korea, Samoa, and Hawaii. This stepped-up involvement took place, however, within the limits set by the Old Paradigm. American involvement was erratic and tentative; it was often amateurish and almost always initiated in the field rather than Washington. Hardly anyone, either at home or abroad, regarded American advances in the Pacific and Asia as essential to the national interest.

Because immigration issues divided Americans, Michael Hunt notes, Washington found it difficult to hew to a coherent Chinese policy. Generally, however, the United States adhered to its "jackal diplomacy," picking up change from the sidewalk after European thugs had rolled the Chinaman

for his bigger cash. Americans cooperated in punitive exped-
itions staged by Britain and France, enforcing the system of
treaties in which the West wrung concessions damaging to
both China's sovereignty and pride. Washington also
exploited its status as a "most favored nation," auto-
matically receiving any commercial concession granted to
another nation. Thus, the United States joined the European
powers in benefiting from open ports, low tariffs, and extraterritorial rights in China.

Although China's rulers did regard the United States as
the most benign and least threatening of Western nations,
Americans eventually flattered themselves with far rosier
images of Chinese admiration and deference. This was not
usually so in the late nineteenth century, however. Americans in China neither adored the Chinese nor nursed illusions about China's view of the United States. In 1883 U.S.
minister John Russell Young lashed out at the Imperial
Court's "eunuchs, . . . pink buttoned censors who read the
stars . . . and all that mass of thieving treacherous, cowardly
cunning adventurers which surround the throne and live an
insectiverous, parasitic existence on this venerable and
august monarchy." At home Sinophobia emerged as a serious social and political problem, especially in the West. A
California GOP leader wrote President Harrison in 1888:
"On this coast to compare a man to a China man is more in-
sulting than to compare him to a '*Nigger*' by far." No
sooner had the 1868 Burlingame Treaty opened the gates to
a large Chinese immigration than a popular cry arose to
close them. By a new treaty of 1880, the United States was
obliged to protect the rights of Chinese already in the country but also allowed to limit or suspend further immigration
in a "reasonable" way. Congress jumped at the chance, in
1882 "suspending" Chinese immigration for a "reasonable"
period of twenty years, amended to ten after President Arthur vetoed the first act. In 1888, following lynchings of
Chinese in Washington Territory and Wyoming, Congress
banned Chinese immigration altogether, thus unilaterally ab-

rogating the 1880 treaty. All the while, Washington demanded respect for its special rights in China.

American influence in Japan slipped after the Civil War because no one cared enough to exploit Commodore Matthew Perry's historic opening of the nation in 1854. The only noteworthy development before the late nineties was the break with other white nations in support of "treaty revision." After several false starts, this decision to give up some extraterritorial rights, returning most control over ports and tariffs to Japan, reached fruition in an 1894 treaty. Washington's voluntary surrender of special rights meant a further decline of influence, but American statesmen either failed to notice or did not care.

Across the Sea of Japan, the United States opened ties with Korea. Most Westerners were baffled by its connection with China, which claimed suzerainty over Korea but no responsibility for her actions. A U.S. naval squadron had vainly attempted to open Korea in 1871, but a decade later the prospects were better. China now looked for an outside power as a counterweight to Japan, which did pry Korea open à la Perry in 1876. The same Captain Shufeldt who had voyaged along the coasts of Africa arrived in China on the USS *Ticonderoga* in 1881. After months of talks with Chinese officials, he completed a treaty in 1882, which he then took to Seoul for the nervous Koreans to sign. Shufeldt's deed came at the end of a route paved by naiveté and incompetence. Shufeldt was oblivious of the ins and outs of Korea's internal affairs and naive about the barriers to friendly relations with the Hermit Kingdom. And Washington had understood too little about East Asian politics to advise him correctly in his original instructions, forcing the ambitious Shufeldt into an unusual degree of ad libbing. He nonetheless got his treaty.

The Treaty of Chemulpo permitted the opening of a U.S. diplomatic mission in Korea and covered standard commercial items. The remarkable things about the treaty were the way it was arrived at and its consequences for U.S.–Korean relations. Shufeldt's first instructions from Washington offered an inadequate map for the maze he encountered; not surprisingly, he exceeded them. When he twice cabled home for help, asking whether he should give in to China's insistence on an endorsement of its special status in Korea, the state department never responded. When he went ahead on his own and refused such an acknowledgement of Korea's dependence on China, neither Shufeldt nor the state department fully realized what a boost he had given Japan in the contest for Korean supremacy. Afterward, Korea's king eagerly looked to the Americans in Seoul for relief from both Chinese and Japanese pressures. Washington, however, was not interested and shrugged off the chance to wield dominant influence in Korea. By 1884, the state department was forcing its own representatives to the sidelines, where they watched helplessly as Japan, China, and Russia jostled for advantage. As in Japan, the United States had forfeited an important foothold. Few at home cared.

Many cared, however, about Hawaii and Samoa. As early as 1842 President John Tyler had declared that the United States could not tolerate a European takeover of Hawaii, already an important stopover in the China trade, American whalers' port, and field for missionaries. After several tentative gestures toward annexation from the 1850s to the early 1870s, America's grip began tightening. The reciprocal trade treaty of 1875, by allowing Hawaiian sugar into the United States duty-free, stimulated sugar cultivation and made the islands an adjunct of the American economy. The treaty also obliged Hawaii never to sell any territory to other nations. The grip intensified in the 1887 renewal of the treaty when the Senate insisted on a provision granting use and control of Pearl Harbor to the United States. In the same year, Washington turned aside an Anglo-French proposal for a three-way guarantee of Hawaiian independence

Slow to Annex

and neutrality. Annexation now seemed inevitable, but the turn of events that brought the islands fully into the American embrace belongs to the account of the 1890s.

Oddly, Americans also grew excited about Samoa, more than four thousand miles from San Francisco in the South Pacific. These islands inspired a surprisingly forward policy. The first Americans on the scene were a shady group of merchants and land speculators, but the excellent harbor of Pago Pago soon attracted official attention, for the navy wanted it. The narrative details from 1872, when the Senate rejected a treaty granting Pago Pago to the United States, until 1899, when the United States and Germany partitioned the islands between themselves, interest only a few specialists—and connoisseurs of comic opera. With Americans named Albert B. Steinberger and Berthild Greenebaum joining a predominantly German cast, with Robert Louis Stevenson fortuitously on hand to write an eyewitness libretto (*A Footnote to History: Eight Years of Trouble in Samoa* [1892]), the show lasted three decades, each act ending with a new Samoan chief saluting the freshly raised flag of either Germany, the United States, or England, his symbolic gesture soon to be irritably disavowed in Berlin, Washington, or London. The climax was the great hurricane of 1889 which, as one would expect in such a script, arrived just as German and American warships maneuvered for possible hostilities, the winds battering both fleets, killing 150 men including 49 Americans, and bringing all the main actors to their senses. Along the way the United States took over Pago Pago in 1878 and joined Britain and Germany in a three-way Samoan condominium in 1889 before, in the last scene, dividing the islands with Germany in 1899 as the British received solace elsewhere. American Samoa would never have the strategic importance expected of it, but the years of intrigue and conflict invested in its acquisition contributed in no small measure to the rise of an expansionist spirit in the United States.

Conc

From the end of the Civil War to the late eighties, the United States conducted its affairs to the beat of irregular drums. Political leaders showed a feckless disdain for diplomacy typical of the times. The state department, for example, closed down its Bogotá legation just as de Lesseps started his Central American canal project. President Rutherford B. Hayes appointed a secretary of the navy who had never sailed on anything larger than a rowboat; when he first boarded a U.S. warship, the secretary yelled out in amazement, "Why, the durned thing's hollow!" Hardly had Shufeldt's treaty been ratified than Congress demoted America's man in Seoul to the lowly rank of minister-resident, without protest from the White House or Foggy Bottom. In 1885 a blue-ribbon commission returned from a tour with a long string of ideas for increasing U.S. trade and influence in Latin America; Congress put out the welcome mat for the commissioners but neglected all their proposals. In 1887 just the idea of creating assistant-secretary posts in the war and navy departments was denounced by newspapers as an intolerable demonstration of militarism.

In this atmosphere, American diplomats were not likely to turn into a corps of foreign policy professionals. Instead, diplomatic posts served as political footballs. In the mid-eighties President Cleveland named an Irish-American named Anthony Keiley as minister to Italy, only to have him blocked by Italian-Americans annoyed by an anti-Italian statement he had uttered. When Austria rejected him both because of the statement and because his wife was Jewish, Cleveland left the Vienna legation empty for two years instead of antagonizing Irish-Americans by giving in to Austria. No less faithful to the Old Paradigm were the presidents who sent famous poets and novelists abroad, not to distinguish themselves as diplomats, but to find something new to write about. Thus, President Garfield, who had enjoyed reading *Ben Hur*, hoped to get another good book from Lew Wallace by shifting him from Paraguay to Turkey.

As William N. Still, Jr., has observed, before the Atlantic cable became available, "squadron and ship commanding officers [frequently] had to make important decisions without reference to Washington." Naval officers' tendency to operate on their own hook, however, stemmed from more than communications problems. Sailing off the coast of Mexico in the 1870s, George Dewey learned that native workers might use violence against U.S.-owned silver mines. Unless the district governor sent troops to quell the disturbance, he threatened to shell a nearby town. According to his biographer, Ronald Spector, Dewey failed to consult with Washington beforehand or report the affair afterward. Usually the navy's independence on the faraway seas turned out harmlessly enough, but officers with their own axes to grind flouted solemn orders during the 1885 intervention in Panama. Ordered to stay neutral but left unsupervised, the navy blatantly took sides, jailing rebel leaders and cooperating with local Colombian officials. Even worse, writes Daniel Wicks, the Cleveland administration "never dealt with the fact that its policies had not been followed," and may never have known this was true.

The center of government usually did not control or even keep track of events. Americans in Madagascar for years accumulated bits of influence and handed out shreds of commitments. Only when France was poised to use force in controlling the island did Washington realize the danger and pull back its people. In China during his world tour in 1879, former president Grant naively offered his services in a subtle Sino-Japanese dispute over the Ryukyu Islands. The Hayes administration learned about this gesture months later—and even tried to follow up on it. The extraordinary Robert Shufeldt in 1879 promised the Sultan of Zanzibar that the United States would rise to his defense should anyone else (France? Britain?) menace his independence. In 1880, as he sailed toward the scene of his Korean negotiations, he ordered the U.S. minister in Japan to open preliminary talks, using the Japanese as go-betweens, an arrangement Washington later acknowledged helplessly. Not that Shufeldt preferred such freedom of action; on the contrary, he complained bitterly during his voyages about Washington's "official inertness." "We seem to be left to our own devices," he wrote in 1879 in West Africa.

In short, as Paul M. Kennedy writes, pre-1890s examples of vigorous American action abroad "were the result of the activities of individual pressure groups, enterprises and statesmen rather than the deliberate choice of the American people themselves or their representatives in Washington." The period discussed in this chapter was marked by a *normal* confusion, by the field's taking the lead because the center had defaulted, and by a policy vacuum in Washington. This formula could at any moment produce the absurd, such as the bizarre events in Hawaii after the death of the queen dowager in 1870. The U.S. consul in Honolulu, wishing to do honor to the deceased, lowered his flag to half staff. The redoubtable Commander William T. Truxtun, however, took offense at this act and led marines and bluejackets in an attack on the consulate so the flag might freely wave again. Nobody in Washington could confidently have said which man had acted correctly.

1. Effects At Home
 - All Expansion Dead

2. Shrinking of modern world.

THREE

From the Old to the New Foreign Policy Paradigm

SUDDEN BLOWS TO THE OLD PARADIGM

A new era in American diplomatic history opened around 1890; the policymaker of 1900 would differ sharply from his predecessor of 1880. An old diplomatic paradigm gave way to a new. What caused this change? What was the character

72

of the New Paradigm? What remnants of the old epoch persisted into the new?

A paradigm shift comes from both a change in conditions ("facts") and the perception of those conditions ("interpretations"). Time itself will usually change things enough to outmode an old paradigm. A policy born in the days of rickety biplanes would probably die before the advent of cruise missiles. When the givens of the past are called into question, they have lost their status as givens, opening the door for successors. Such a shift can happen even when "objective" circumstances change very little if people begin seeing them from a radically different angle. It can be argued, for instance, that the big change in Cuba from the 1870s to the 1890s was how it looked to Americans. Hamilton Fish's contemporaries were ready to stand by while Spain harried the rebels into submission; William McKinley's, in comparable circumstances, were not. This change in *perception*, Alan Henrikson observes, will lead to a paradigm shift only if a new *conception* is available as a substitute. Crises in old paradigms, however, can usually be counted on to stimulate the birth of new ones. Certainly this was true in the late nineteenth century, when altered circumstances and outlook combined to produce a shift in diplomatic paradigms.

Diplomatic paradigms are unlikely to change as suddenly as Thomas Kuhn's scientific paradigms. But the paradigm dominant in the quarter century after 1865 did fall abruptly, suggesting that some sudden and severe shocks joined the erosion of passing time in accelerating the transition from old to new. Three sudden blows, closely related, were most responsible for triggering the paradigm shift and diplomatic "revolution" of the nineties. Two occurred at home, one abroad. The first was a widespread social malaise that plunged Americans into a state of anxiety and gloom in the late eighties and early nineties. The second was a severe economic crisis and depression in the mid-nineties, which deepened the malaise. The third was an unexpected threat to

U.S. export markets in Europe and China, a shock magnified in importance by the two other blows.

The Social Malaise

Many Americans in the eighties and nineties found themselves in a fog of uneasiness, a confusion about the present and fear for the nation's future. At the center of this cloud, called the "psychic crisis" of the nineties by Richard Hofstadter, was a sudden decline in popular confidence. The viability of American institutions seemed in doubt. Many, especially from older English and German stocks, suspected that the American "race" was deteriorating in quality. Intellectuals and other opinion makers in particular sensed with a chill that American society was no longer moving along its preordained path to bigger and better things, but had somehow been cast adrift.

Several concrete changes led to this intangible discomfort. One was the transformation in U.S. demography. The rapid growth of population from 39 million in 1870 to 63 million in 1890 was unsettling enough (a comparable rise would have brought America's 1960 population of 179 million up to 289 million by 1980, instead of 225 million). The makeup of the growth seemed even more disturbing; more than half a million immigrants arrived on American shores annually in the 1880s. Many saw in such figures a menace to social homogeneity and national solidarity, especially because of the dramatic shift occurring in the sources of immigration from northern and western to southern and eastern Europe. The new people looked and seemed different in the eyes of the "natives." As Russian Jews, Poles, Italians, and Greeks streamed into the country (instead of more familiar Germans and Norwegians), the old-line social groups thought they could feel the foundation of their society shifting under their feet.

Another development of the eighties and nineties that made the time seem out of joint was the astonishing growth of American cities. Unready for expansion and poorly governed, these had almost overnight become home for millions of immigrants and uprooted farmers. Thomas Jefferson had predicted social disaster if America's yeoman society were ever replaced by a nation of city-dwellers. As the countryside emptied and urban problems multiplied, he looked more and more like a prophet.

The growth of business "trusts" and labor unions dealt another blow to American tranquility. Both the rapidly growing trust movement and the rising number and militancy of labor unions were unfamiliar. Middle-class entrepeneurs, aspiring young professionals, and old-style artisans felt caught between the millstones of organized economic power. They came to believe that the doors of opportunity had suddenly closed to the common man. In the land of opportunity, this was no small thing. Why was there a "Sugar Trust" when every man should have a slice of the pie? How had the Senate become a club of millionaires? Could an Abe Lincoln still become president?

Then the mid-nineties brought a new parade of horrors. The ugly face of class conflict leered in scenes wrought by the crushing panic and depression of 1893–97. America seemed to explode in violence and radicalism. Amid the turmoil of the Homestead Strike, Pullman Boycott, Coxey's March, and Free Silver, educated Americans spoke fearfully of a new Jacobin Revolution or the fall of a latter-day Rome. In an 1893 address the young historian Frederick Jackson Turner made a notable attempt to explain some of these changes in American life. America's first epoch had ended with the passing of its frontier experience, to which Turner traced America's national character, democratic government, and, implicitly, economic prosperity. A frontierless future looked unpromising. Other writers popularized the "where-do-we-go-from-here?" strain in Turner's thesis. Before long a public speaker was judged remiss if he failed to address the problems of a nation that had lost its frontier safety valve. Although Turner barely hinted at the thought, many pundits warned that the United States would face shrinking opportunities and mushrooming social crises unless its people found a new frontier to absorb their dynamic energies and support their traditional way of life—a frontier of export markets and colonies.

These waves of doubt about America's strength, health, and purpose produced some unpredictable results. One, Richard Hofstadter suggested, was a burst of energy directed both inward and outward. The energy coursing through campaigns for social and political reform reassured Americans of their continuing vitality. The short-tempered jingoism of the era came from a need to reaffirm American strength: the United States could thrash some other country in a war or, more subtly, demonstrate its ability to govern "inferior" peoples in an empire. Once indifferent to the outside world because they were too busy building their own society, Americans now scanned the seas and other lands in search of reassurance.

The social malaise of the late eighties and early nineties pried open grudging minds to disturbing new ideas; the old ones were found wanting. In an era of drastic social change, old maxims lost their sway over people who could take them for granted no longer. Calm and thoughtful Americans, as well as those who were baffled or scared, felt forced by events to reexamine the precepts of U.S. foreign policy. Maybe Washington's and Jefferson's warnings against foreign entanglements were wrong, or inapplicable to modern times. Perhaps the old taboo against colonies now stood in the way of progress, even of safety. Accepted givens were no longer "given."

The Panic and Depression

America's malaise intensified, and drew more people into its gloomy embrace, when a shattering panic and depression struck in 1893. The crisis arrived just as factories began to outdo farms, mines, and forests in the value of American exports, and just before America outstripped Britain as the world's greatest industrial nation. The depression, therefore, not only deepened the malaise by further eroding American optimism; it also sounded to many like an urgent and cruel signal that both economy and society required a massive increase in sales abroad. This notion, however *Need to Export* dubious in hindsight, was accepted in the nineties as true by businessmen, politicians, and publicists alike. The traditional American interest in foreign trade now took on obsessive proportions. Trade could no longer be handled so casually but now demanded continuous and systematic attention at the highest levels of the state.

The Threat to Old Markets

The export problem appeared urgent by the early nineties; by 1897 and 1898 it seemed almost desperate. European governments abruptly raised tariffs against U.S. imports in both their own territories and colonies. After the *Tariffs* Sino-Japanese war of 1894–95, victorious Japan and the great powers of Europe descended on the ancient empire in such a whirlwind of annexations and spheres of influence that the utter disappearance of a sovereign China seemed possible. How was the United States to survive the emergency of the nineties if, while scrambling for new markets, other powers suddenly carved up China? What would happen if reliable old customers suddenly vanished behind new tariff walls raised against American products on the continent and throughout the British empire? Experts widely shared the view that the United States must either take decisive *diplomatic* action or suffer economic (and thus social) disaster.

THE IMPACT OF CUMULATIVE CHANGE

Thus a series of abrupt dislocations helped to spark a reevaluation of diplomatic axioms. Where once Americans had seen social stability, prosperity, and open foreign markets, they now viewed social disorder, a catastrophic depression, and iron shutters rolled down against American tradesmen. Although these sudden and unforeseen developments were essential in toppling the Old Paradigm, they were not sufficient to the task. Other factors—slow-working and cumulative—had been undermining the old givens for a long time.

National Growth and Progress

The thirty years that passed after the Civil War left an indelible mark on U.S. foreign policy. Economic growth, for instance, produced not only a bothersome surplus but greater American influence in international affairs. The average American's awareness of the country's growing wealth and numbers reshaped attitudes toward the rest of the world. As a Connecticut senator told a reporter in 1893: "A policy of isolation did well enough when we were an embryo nation, but today things are different. . . . We are sixty-five million of people, the most advanced and powerful on earth, and regard to our future welfare demands an abandonment of the doctrines of isolation."

Technological advances, too, had their effect. Progress in transportation and communication produced a shrinking and more accessible world, an alluring vision to ambitious men. Distant events also seemed more likely to impinge on American interests, calling for a more security-minded foreign policy. Though long ago noting the commercial and military significance of steam power, most historians have overlooked the impact of the telegraphic cables laid in the oceans during the late nineteenth century. This new communication system tied distant markets together and stimulated political leaders to thoughts of expansion: "Commerce follows the cables," Henry Cabot Lodge wrote in 1898. As James A. Field, Jr., has written, as the net of cables grew, it became "possible to administer modernity . . . at previously unheard-of distances."

The cable also meant that governments could rapidly

make contact with their ministers and ambassadors, thus accelerating diplomacy. Crises could both start and end with breathtaking speed, which made the world seem more dangerous. The ability of central governments to dictate fleet movements according to plan, as well as other changes in the art and artifacts of war, made the United States seem more vulnerable to foreign attack. Army officers added France, Germany, and Japan to their list of potential battlefield enemies (along with Britain and Spain). From 1889 to the mid-nineties, James Abrahamson writes, they "expressed fear of European imperialism, a future struggle for control of an isthmian canal, and commercial rivalries that might lead to a challenge to the Monroe Doctrine." The assumption—the given—that the United States faced no serious international danger, which lay at the heart of the Old Paradigm, had been shattered.

Threats

Naval officers, too, found the future worrisome. In 1889 Captain Mahan brooded about a German threat to the United States, hoping that the Samoan crisis had "roused [Americans] from sleep. . . ." A year later an officer at the War College predicted that U.S. isolation would soon "cease to exist," replaced by a "sharp commercial competition with others in every part of the world" that could lead to war. And since technology appeared to promise a future of short but devastating wars, navy Captain Charles Stockton observed in 1893, the future's losers would be those unready for immediate combat—the American military's chronic condition. New weapons took a long time to build and little time to do their destruction. If the United States failed to prepare for war long in advance, it might be routed, perhaps never to recover. The militia spirit of the Minuteman must be abandoned; both army and navy officers believed their services were in a "crisis."

Build up

A New Generation

The fading away of the Civil War generation also influenced the paradigm change. Although they might occasionally tell their old campfire stories or dust off their uniforms, both Blue and Gray veterans were cool to further adventure and sacrifice. They remembered the inglorious realities of war and knew how many lives it had ruined. They were chagrined at the war's disappointing legacy of racial and political problems. A Boston publisher, wounded at the hands of the Confederates, wrote during the Venezuela crisis of 1895–96: "I have . . . seen enough of war and its effects to induce me to use every effort in my power to prevent the spread of any desire for war with any country." These men, whose tithe of strife and selflessness had been paid in full, plunged singlemindedly into the favorite new sport of moneymaking. By the early nineties, however, a new group of men was rising to power: these were men unimpressed by commercial values, inexperienced in moral crusades, and with no war to call their own, especially the kind found depicted in their parents' parlor magazines. In 1898 one of these new men, Theodore Roosevelt, would tell Civil War veteran and anti-imperialist Carl Schurz, "you and your generation have had your chance from 1861 to 1865. Now let us of this generation have ours!"

Nationalism

Shifting streambeds of ideas and attitudes also helped change the course of American diplomacy. Imperial powers are rarely deficient in *amour-propre*, and few periods of U.S. history were as noisily nationalistic as the 1890s. Patriotic societies and historical groups sprouted on all sides. An "Americanization" movement initiated recent immigrants into the customs and glories of their adopted nation, while their children were baptized in patriotism by the public schools. This chauvinistic fervor displeased sophisticates, such as the editorial writer in the *New York Journal of Commerce*, who complained in 1895 that, "This rage of displaying the flag in season and out of season, this remarkable fashion of hanging the flag over every schoolhouse and of giving boys military drill, and this passion for tracing one's ancestry to somebody who fought in the Revolutionary War or the War of 1812, or at least against the French and Indians, all help to create a false spirit of militarism.'' In three years' time American militarism would find a live target.

Imperialist Thought

Surges of nationalism had appeared before, as in the 1820s, without being channeled into imperialism. What distinguished the nineties' wave of popular nationalism was the imperialist thinking carried along in the surf. In recent years, historians have shown that the "imperialism" of some thinkers has been exaggerated, such as naval strategist Alfred T. Mahan, geopolitician Brooks Adams, and missionary spokesman Josiah Strong. But though their views may have been twisted in the retelling, the paths they charted certainly led in the direction of imperialism. Probably the most important of these men was Mahan, whose *The Influence of Seapower upon History* was published in 1890. James A. Field, Jr., and others have reemphasized the defensive character of his pre-1898 strategic writings. Nonetheless, Mahan fired a deadly salvo of books and articles against the navy's obsession with defending coastlines and raiding enemy merchants. If the United States was to be a great power, it must have a navy capable of carrying the battle, defensive or otherwise, directly to the enemy's war fleet. Mahan believed in the importance of foreign markets to America's future, and in time he became convinced that she was justified in dominating unproductive peoples. Although never presented as a program, Mahan's preferences added up to expanding exports, acquiring a few colonies to supply raw materials and markets for American industry, building a swift and modern navy to protect America's overseas possessions and shipping lanes, and supporting the navy with an isthmian canal and control of coaling and repair bases in the Pacific and East Asia. Many Americans found such ideas exhilarating.

Few historians any longer think that high-brow intellectuals believing in a doctrine called "Social Darwinism" wielded much influence in late-nineteenth-century foreign policy circles. It remains apparent, however, that boiled-down versions of this "ism" became a staple of expansionist thought. By defining struggle as the primary engine of progress and survival, Social Darwinism, however popularized, spread the message of the vigorous life and warned the nation against living for peace and prosperity. The United States in turning soft would become easy prey for tougher peoples. Social Darwinism also offered new respectability to racism, especially the idea that the world's peoples consisted of greater and lesser breeds. If Asian, African, or even Latin American peoples could not fend off the great imperial powers, they merely exposed their unfitness in the struggle for existence. Ruling such peoples in colonies, therefore, could be seen as a generous act rather than a violation of American principles. This rationale for imperialism grew popular just as Northerners gave up on the ex-slaves, deciding they had to be returned at least temporarily to the safekeeping of southern whites. Thus Social Darwinism both fed from the growing disenchantment with Reconstruction and reinforced it.

A first cousin of Social Darwinism was "Anglo-Saxonism," which also prepared American minds for imperialism. Anglo-Saxons, according to this view, stood on the top rung of the evolutionary ladder, uniquely qualified for an imperial role because of their superiority in the art of government. Although a puzzling idea to arise during an era of American political corruption—this "ism," of course, may have provided a timely reassurance—Anglo-Saxonism further justified expansionist policies. It also encouraged Americans to believe they were more suited for imperial roles than other such undeniably "fit" nations as Germany and Russia.

Missionaries

American missionaries did much to arouse expansionist sentiment. A Methodist clergyman who had visited Puerto Rico in 1900 reported on the progress already being made because of religious services "in neat, attractive churches, with plenty of good singing . . . with Sunday school, young people's societies, etc. . . ." The desire to carry God's Message to the heathen (often the Protestant Message to Catholics) grew phenomenally. From 1870 to 1900 foreign Protestant missions established by Americans jumped 500 percent; from 1890 to 1900 American missionaries in China rose from 513 to more than a thousand. Aside from fundraising campaigns, which publicized their crusades in thousands of church basements, missionaries willy-nilly stimulated the growth of American expansionism. Their presence abroad boosted U.S. exports by exposing "natives" to American goods, which the missionaries ordered from home for their own needs. Missionaries also made profits for merchants at home by preachment of morality abroad (draping aborigines' nakedness with New England textiles or encouraging Christian frugality by perusading Samoans to save up for Singer sewing machines). Generally, as Milton Plesur has noted, missionaries' experiences eroded parochialism, opening the way for the growth of internationalism and concern for the lives (as well as souls) of distant peoples.

The New American Mission

In effect, the missionaries were the first converts to a new definition of the American mission. By the 1890s many thoughtful Americans had grown unhappy with the quietist notion that the United States should provide a model, but nothing more, for others. At a time when the world was smaller and more hazardous than ever and America's moral and material superiority seemed nearly an established fact rather than a distant goal, the passivity of the old idea of mission looked like both a dangerous luxury and a selfish abnegation of duty. "The mission of this country," former secretary of state Richard Olney wrote in 1898, "is not merely to pose but to act . . . to forego no fitting opportunity to further the progress of civilization." The Wilsonian vision of saving the world for democracy lurked just around the corner. In the meantime, American ideology had taken a step that resonated with imperialist potential.

Journalism and Information

Americans who remained unseduced by these strategic and ideological novelties often found it hard to hold their own because of their sparse knowledge of the outside world. Although they might draw crowds with orations on American traditions and principles, they knew little about places like China or Hawaii. The reading public, greatly enlarged by educational advances and with access to a greater supply of cheap and informative magazines and newspapers, learned more than ever about foreign regions, usually from writers favoring a more forward-looking U.S. diplomacy. Journalism on the Far East, for instance, improved markedly after the Sino-Japanese War. "In the earlier period," Marilyn B. Young states, "journals carried fairly regular articles describing the customs, manners and general oddities of the mysterious Orient. From 1894 on, these capsule culture essays virtually disappear," replaced by "political, social, and economic reports and analyses by a new group of amateur and professional Far Eastern experts." The new journalism helped prepare the way for the New Paradigm.

THE NEW PARADIGM

The net effect of these many developments—both gradual and sudden, external and internal—was to change circumstances and outlook, producing a new epoch in American foreign policy. The American people had not only come to

live in a world much altered in recent times, but also to view
their world, including what had not changed, from a radically transformed perspective. They were like valley
dwellers forced to the mountain top by a flood: they could
see that the river itself had changed course, as other topographical features had been redrawn by the waters; but the
abandoned village, though undamaged by the deluge, also
looked remarkably different from the new mountain vantage
point. The New Paradigm was the product of just such a
combination of altered landscape and novel perspective, as
we shall see from examining its component parts.

The Idea of World Power

Under this new paradigm, Americans thought of their
nation not merely as a great moral force, but as a world
power obliged to act like one. Only a few years earlier U.S.
ministers had agonized about how best to maintain a simple
"republican" style in their residences, clothing, and conver-
sations. Now, with a new formality and solemnity, they bent
themselves to protecting America's interests and to increasing her influence with other nations. This new consciousness
of American strength and importance found perfect symbolic
expression in the behavior of the U.S. commissioners at the
first session of the Paris peace talks with Spain in the
autumn of 1898. One U.S. delegate, Whitelaw Reid, recorded the event for his diary: ". . . we all entered the large
room. Secretary [of State William] Day was taking a place
on the side facing the windows, when some of our Commissioners beckoned to him to take the other side, evidently
preferring to make the Spaniards face the light."

Expansion of Interests

Americans, now acutely conscious of their strength, not
only rubbed salt in the wounds of a former power now fallen
on hard times; everywhere they watched they saw events
important to American interests. They scrutinized such tradi-

tional centers of attention as Canada, Mexico, Cuba, and Hawaii, but now they also worried about Nicaragua, Venezuela, Brazil, Chile, China, the Philippines, and even (momentarily) Turkish Armenia. In the easygoing days of the Old Paradigm only a crank would have seen anything "vital" to the United States much beyond the horizons of the nation's borders; in the 1890s levelheaded Americans keenly felt threats to U.S. interests halfway around the world. By 1895, Michael Hunt writes, American "policy makers were as resolute in keeping China in line as they had been earlier in keeping hands off." Other governments were quick to notice the difference: after its near-clash with Washington over Samoa in 1889, Berlin, now looking on the United States as a competing colonial power with expanding interests, began designing plans for a future war with the new world nation. Like young men who had put away their toy guns for real weapons, American policymakers put gentler times behind and girded themselves for a long struggle with what they took to be harsh reality.

Policy

Theodore Roosevelt's friend, Henry Cabot Lodge, once drew a line between a nation's "foreign relations" and its "foreign policy," remarking then that Washington had little need for the latter. But safeguarding interests newly defined as vital in wider parts of a dangerous world did require a "foreign policy," and its appearance may have been the most important development of the New Paradigm. A "policy" approach meant bringing several new features into the practice of diplomacy. One was continuity, both spatial and temporal. Abrupt and casual shifts in U.S. policies diminished in the 1890s. Grover Cleveland, for instance, repeatedly ditched Arthur's initiatives during his first term in the eighties, but mainly sustained Benjamin Harrison's in the nineties: the navy yards still rang with the clamor of building a new battle fleet; officials stayed on the lookout for European incursions in hemispheric latitudes. And had Cleveland's term lasted beyond 1897, he probably would have gone to war over Cuba just as McKinley did, for the New York Democrat and Ohio Republican pursued almost identical Cuban policies. Policymakers now identified specific and important interests abroad and designed definite plans to protect and advance them. Self-consciousness about the international scene, which Akira Iriye believes increased throughout the world at this time, produced more clearly defined interests and more continuity in the formation and execution of policy. System began to replace spasm.

"Policy" also meant a new awareness of the interlacing of issues. The Bering Straits on Tuesday and Hawaii on Wednesday, with a briefing book for each placed on the secretary of state's desk, was not the way Washington later began doing things. In the nineties officials acted forcefully in Cuba partly to impress the European imperial powers in China with America's strength and determination. Having identified major American interests in East Asia, they saw the necessity of annexing Hawaii, strengthening the navy, and increasing its mobility by acquiring a Central American canal route. Finally, they came to terms with Great Britain on future canal rights and then sought to protect those rights by more closely scrutinizing the conduct of European powers in the Caribbean.

Another sign of the switch to "policy" was the increased willingness of officials to risk moving beyond what public opinion supported, if this seemed necessary to protect American interests. They might also defy public opinion, or, alternatively, create and shape public opinion where none had existed. Although amateurish in technique by later standards, three consecutive administrations—those of Harrison, Cleveland, and McKinley—aroused friendly editors and congressmen to generate public support in, respectively, the attempted annexation of Hawaii in 1893, the handling of the Venezuelan affair in 1895, and the dispatch of U.S. infantry to the Philippines immediately after Dewey's victory at Manila. In none of these cases had the public demanded what the government did; in all of them officials had outstripped the concerns of the American people.

The development of "policy" brought with it a historic shift in initiative from the field to the center. Although, as James A. Field suggests, the ability to send messages back and forth along the new cable networks helped expedite this change, Washington's control had always been available for the asking. Only when a new era's perceived needs demanded centralized attention and energy did it come about. Thus, Marilyn B. Young writes, in China until about 1895 individual Americans, "diplomats, missionaries, adventurers . . . acted independently of government direction in the belief that personal efforts could have a direct effect on the destiny of nations, even empires. . . ." Now, however, "strong government backing" seemed necessary, "not the heroic efforts of an individual, and bold schemes on the part of restless Americans disappeared. Government initiative replaced that of the individual and, by the end of the first decade of the twentieth century, roles had been so far reversed that the government found itself looking for individual support rather than the other way around." Diplomats abroad acutely felt this role reversal. Formerly in the cockpit of action precisely because they were in the field, beyond a somnolent government's reach, they were now reined in with a jerk. Secretary of State John Sherman in 1897, for example, instructed the new U.S. minister to Korea, where American agents had long ignored Washington, that he was not a "counselor" to Seoul; reminding him that the United States had no "protective alliance" with Korea, he starchily warned him to maintain "absolute neutrality" in its affairs. Missionaries, too, were affected. Formerly, American missionaries in China had been inclined to take the initiative, frequently to the annoyance of state department officials. But the 1890s, Michael Hunt states, "brought a major and lasting shift in policy favorable to the mission movement. By the end of the decade Washington had dramatically broadened its definition of missionary rights and demonstrated its willingness to defend the exercise of those rights, even in the face of undiminished Chinese opposition." An analogous switch in initiative occurred in economic affairs, not only from the field to Washington, but from private to public hands. In 1889 the secretary of agriculture implored the state department to take "especial pains" in encouraging U.S. consuls to ferret out new markets for American farm commodities; in 1897 the department ordered consuls to give equal attention to "extending the sales of American manufacturers"; on New Year's Day in 1898 the department began publishing the *Daily Consular Reports*. The diplomatic conduct of the United States, though still often timid by European standards, was beginning to reflect the nation's new international ambitions.

In their most ambitious moments, American officials now modestly began calculating their country's place in the balance of power, and even trying to tip the balance for the sake of American interests. Other ambitious goals might require a willingness to intervene in the internal affairs of other nations, a sign of a country that takes its foreign policy seriously indeed. As Assistant Secretary of State John Bassett Moore wrote in 1899, the United States had moved "from a position of comparative freedom from entanglements into the position of what is commonly called a world power. . . . Where formerly we had only commercial interests, we now have territorial and political interests as well." Perhaps the greatest sign of a nation's seriousness in foreign affairs is the willingness to use force in policy's behalf. By this standard, too, the United States government—increasingly ready to use the navy and army when diplomacy failed—had broken with the past.

Instruments of Foreign Affairs

If American institutions were to implement a foreign policy with a frontier of defense extending from the Windward Passage to the Heavenly City of Peking, they would have to change. The foreign service did change—slightly. Congress authorized the rank of ambassador in 1893; consuls redirected their energies from assuring the payment of duties on goods imported into the United States to promoting the exports of American goods into the countries in which they served.

Changes in the military, though more substantial, were not aimed at creating an American empire. James Abrahamson has shown that military reformers, impressed by the world's dangers, aimed at more rational decision making, continuity of policy, and centralized control of the services. They brought about "concentration of the combat forces, improved officer education, and periodic maneuvers—all of which would enhance the services' readiness for war." Congress finally voted funds to fortify the U.S. coastline, now thought of as vulnerable to attack. The army founded an intelligence service in 1885 and four years later conducted its first elaborate maneuvers. Located in Indian Territory (Oklahoma), the three-week operation came to be known as the "Bloody War of 1889."

But the greatest changes by far occurred in the navy, which manifested the commodores' new awareness of hazardous times ahead. It was apt, if coincidental, that Alfred T. Mahan's great book, *The Influence of Seapower in History*, appeared early in Benjamin F. Tracy's seminal stewardship of the navy department. Tracy's first annual report in 1889 declared that in future wars the nation "to strike the first blow will gain an advantage . . . and inflict an injury from which [an antagonist] can never recover." Resting content with the old navy, therefore, would be a "fatal mistake." In 1892, concerned about foreign powers' "aggressive" policies, he warned that, "whether it will or not, [the United States] will soon be forced into a position where it cannot disregard measures which form a menace to its prosperity and security." Oddly, as Benjamin F. Cooling's book on Tracy makes clear, farsighted continuity (an aspect of "policy") in naval construction, which required a long lead time, was necessary to defend against the destructive power of the sudden event. Congress, not inquiring into such ironies, supported Tracy as he took charge. He tightened control of policy, administration, and operations. In his own words, he got the old bureau heads to act "with a promptness unexampled in the history of naval administration in this Country." The reform momentum gathered steam. Having already changed its internal code, the navy sent intelligence-gathering attachés abroad for the first time in 1889. Most important, as noted in the previous chapter, this was the navy that ordered its first true battleships in 1890, ships designed to carry the war to the enemy. Capping this era, Congress in 1899 declared that all future battleships should possess "great radius of action" and the navy excised the term "coast-line battleship" from its vocabulary in 1900, the same year it established a general staff for strategy and planning.

Limitations of the New Paradigm

The change described was incomplete. As (Lincoln P.) Bloomfield's Law has it, "Nothing happens until it has to," and Americans found that much could wait until later. Old patterns of conduct and thought persisted. The 1890s might best be understood as transitional, removed in character from the age of Hayes and Garfield but no less than from the age of Woodrow Wilson. One sign was the restrictive geography of the New Paradigm. The American "defense perimeter" of 1900 may have extended to the China Sea, but it did not reach the English Channel, nor certainly the Rhine. The Mideast was blithely ignored; the commander of U.S. naval forces in the Mediterranean told the state department in 1897: "The Department can hardly realize the paucity of American interests in the Levant." Africa was still the Dark Continent, and hands off purely European affairs remained unchallenged as a maxim of U.S. diplomacy. The New Paradigm applied almost exclusively to relations with Latin America and East Asia.

These limitations confirm that diplomatic paradigms reflect obsessions and fantasies every bit as much as so-called facts. Hindsight clearly reveals that American security and business interests in 1898 still hinged on events in Europe, not Asia. American cable-builders had not even put down a line to East Asia. Yet, for men who viewed world affairs through the paradigm filter of the time, the Far East most dazzled the eyes. Marilyn B. Young observes that Americans in the 1890s "somehow came to feel that having influence in Asia was a categorical imperative for a world power." America was a world power, therefore it must take a key part in Far Eastern affairs despite an insufficiency of concrete interests that might impel and support such a role. Before, relations with nearly all foreign nations had been minimized; now, U.S. relations with the Far East were radically altered and her traditional concern with Latin America intensified, but relations with Europe and Africa remained for most purposes unchanged.

The new approach to foreign policy provoked scowls or yawns from many. The mid-nineties depression not only inspired a new emphasis on boosting exports, but many other panaceas as well—protectionism, trade unionism, socialism, free silver, and evangelical revivalism, to name a few. Some of the most astute businessmen and politicians doubted the wisdom of the new departure, and the people at large so little recognized its merit that officials disguised their purposes in the rhetorical garb of the Old Paradigm. Executives more than legislators responded to the paradigm change. Congress, which the *Nation* in 1896 still believed handled diplomatic issues with "puerile levity," often dug in its heels against the new order, scrapping important trade agreements and challenging other novelties. Many supporters of naval building were not dedicated Mahanites at all but understood that reconstruction would sound a healthy din in local shipyards, fire the hearths in underused steel mills, or cost enough tax money to justify holding up tariff rates. The anti-imperialists in and out of Congress rejected the new diplomatic order out of hand.

Although some abler diplomats began serving abroad during the nineties, professionalization of the diplomatic service would wait on the twentieth century. Many ministers remained distinctly amateurish, even those in crucial posts. Election-minded presidents did the appointing. McKinley flooded the consular service with patronage appointees and sent politically deserving nondescripts to several important foreign posts. Politics also moved his hand when he signed commissions for the bumbling Russell Alger to become secretary of war and the semisenile John Sherman secretary of state. Nor did the state department itself change much before the end of the century. Congress refused to authorize consular reform, and according to Richard H. Werking the department in Washington made unimpressive progress in exerting control over agents in the field. When Elihu Root became secretary of state in 1905, he lamented that he was "like a man trying to conduct the business of a large metropolitan law-firm in the office of a village squire." The consular service, he declared, was a place "to shelve broken down politicians and to take care of failures in American life . . . at government expense."

Behavior, more than rhetoric, is the real measure of a paradigm, and at times in the 1890s American behavior in foreign affairs was as diffuse, timid, and inept as ever. Even though the era closed with control of a new empire, Washington's approach afterward to these allegedly essential possessions was lax, almost forgetful. Even in China, so elevated in diplomatic status, the conduct of the newcomers to world power seemed halting and inexpert compared to the Europeans—partly, Robert Wiebe has noticed, because American merchants searching for profits and diplomats for influence rarely talked to each other. Nor was the United States ready to take significant risks in the use of force. Although Washington willingly engaged in rough play against the Chinese and Filipinos (and the hapless Spaniards), it never thought of unsheathing its sword against Japan or major European powers active in Asia. Sometimes American leaders feared they had gotten in over their heads, especially during the U.S.-Philippines War and the Boxer Rebellion. During the complex multinational negotiations that followed the latter, America's chief delegate, W. W. Rockhill, wrote: "I am sick and tired of the whole business and heartily glad to get away from it. . . . England has her agreement with Germany, Russia has her alliance with France, and the Triple Alliance comes in here [China], and every other combination you know of is working here just as it is in Europe. I trust it may be a long time before the United States gets into another muddle of this description." This reads more like the sighs of an Old Paradigm holdover than an architect of the New Paradigm. Like many Americans of the time, he was probably something of both.

Still, American foreign policy had changed significantly by the early nineties. Officials now thought of the United States as a major, even imperial power. Hence the need to have "policies." A powerful navy was essential. So too was a Far Eastern policy—all major powers had one. Asia looked different from its earlier appearance. Having not bothered before to extend cable lines across the Pacific, in 1899 the navy would suddenly demand Wake Island as an "imperative" landing place. It did not matter that what policymakers saw were often mirages. Michael Hunt writes that America's "new outlook [on China] rested on only the flimsiest concrete economic or strategic justification. . . . Its appeal, otherwise inexplicable, has to be understood in terms of the vision that both drew from and fed back into . . . national fantasies. . . ." Similarly, Paul M. Kennedy in *The Samoan Tangle* (1974) contends that "the later stages of imperialism in the nineteenth century were 90 per cent illusion and 10 per cent reality." Deluded or no, the American people were suddenly entreated by officials not to take

George Washington's Farewell Address too literally. They still preferred to act unilaterally but now would cooperate with other powers—especially an increasingly respectful England—if it seemed advantageous. Once wedded to noninterventionism, Americans now put their oar in waters everywhere—in Samoa, Chile, Hawaii, Brazil, Nicaragua, Venezuela, Cuba, Puerto Rico, the Philippines, and China.

Symbolic of the change in American policy is the Asiatic Squadron of the United States Navy, which had three obsolete ships on station in 1889, but patrolled forty-two by 1902. And it was more than symbolic that while no U.S. troops were serving outside the national boundaries in 1870, in 1880, or in 1890, they were fighting, standing guard, and even performing the duties of government in Cuba, Puerto Rico, the Philippines, and China by 1900. A new day had dawned.

FOUR

Early Years of
the New Era,
1889–1897

BENJAMIN HARRISON

The administration of President Benjamin Harrison, which
came into office in March 1889, bore many of the earmarks
of the New Paradigm. The president and his secretaries of
state, James G. Blaine and John W. Foster (John Foster Dul-
les's grandfather), barely dampened their toes in the turbu-

lent waters of East Asia, but in the Western Hemisphere and
Central Pacific they plunged spiritedly into the deep. Harrison, a shrewd and unfriendly little lawyer from Indiana, was
unquestionably in charge. Although his biographers have
never explained how he came to acquire such a command of
the foundations of empire, acquire it he did. Aided by unusual bipartisan support in Congress, he led by force of
ideas and purpose, not personality. From the start he determined to find "larger markets," especially for agricultural
products; Blaine described the administration's objectives as
the "annexation of trade."

Harrison singlemindedly pursued commercial rather than
colonial goals. His inquiet conscience on questions of means
prevented any Grantlike policy of "grab" (and helps explain
his anti-imperialism in 1900). "You know I am not much of
an annexationist," he wrote Blaine in 1891, "though I do
feel that in some directions, as to naval stations and points
of influence, we must look forward to a departure from the
too conservative opinions which have been held heretofore."
Apparently he had in mind acquiring a few harbors and islands in the Caribbean and the Pacific that would guard the
approaches to a future isthmian canal. Harrison and Blaine
ran a government with unusually clear goals, yet as it turned
out their carefully laid plans eventually broke up on the
shoals of unplanned incidents.

Trade and Ports

Harrison and Blaine enjoyed substantial success in refit-
ting the navy, much less in raising the level of exports.
Under navy secretary Benjamin Tracy, the Naval War College supplied the classroom where Captain Mahan could in-
doctrinate young officers. Construction kept pace: the U.S.
Navy ranked between twelfth and seventeenth among the
world's navies in 1889, seventh and still rising by 1893. Attempts to obtain a canal and bases, however, failed. In 1891
Harrison asked Congress to guarantee bonds for an Ameri-

can firm recently set up to build a Nicaraguan canal, but nothing came of the venture. Only the 1889 arrangement for a harbor in Samoa emerged from the flurry of efforts to obtain naval bases, and the credit for that belongs to the Cleveland administration. Negotiations to lease the Peruvian port of Chimbote stalled when Peru asked for protectoratelike guarantees of its territory. Talks again slowed while Washington measured the after-tremors of the 1891-92 crisis with neighboring Chile (see below); the negotiations were finally dissolved by neglect. In the Caribbean, the administration toyed with reviving Seward's old plans for the Danish West Indies and tried without success to lease Samaná Bay in the Dominican Republic. Harrison and Blaine came closest to achieving their goal in Haiti.

Not without getting embroiled in a local civil war, as events turned out. Grover Cleveland, annoyed by French ties with the supposedly legitimate government of Haiti, had flirted with rebels in the north. Their leader, Florvil Hyppolite, had once hinted of a reward for U.S. help in the form of the port of Môle St. Nicholas, which commands the strategic Windward Passage between Haiti and Cuba. Early in the Harrison administration, Washington made sharp demands on the southern regime, was rebuffed, and then watched with satisfaction as supplies reached Hyppolite from the United States and he seized control in October 1889. Now the United States would receive its dividend. In power, however, Hyppolite was no longer the suppliant of leaner times. Assuming that Harrison was bluffing, he stalled in the face of Blaine's pressure and a show of U.S. naval force early in 1891. Hyppolite was right. Harrison did not choose to use naked force and this fiasco, described by Benjamin F. Cooling as resembling "a bungled, amateurish plot," ended with Môle St. Nicholas still Haitian. Harrison and Blaine rejected Portugal's offer of naval facilities in Lisbon, the Azores, Angola, or Mozambique: this administration knew what it wanted (if not always how to get it), and none of the proposed locations fit its overall strategy.

Pan American mkt

Ambitious plans to expand U.S. exports in the hemisphere were designed not only to promote the American economy, but to forestall European political encroachments. Little was accomplished. One reason Americans exported so little to Latin America was the pathetic condition of their merchant shipping. Harrison offered a remedy by asking Congress to grant subsidies to mail-carrying ships and bounties to vessels built in the United States for use in foreign commerce. Congress in response put in place only a modest mail subsidy. A more promising event was the Pan-American conference of 1889–90, the first of its kind ever held. The Democrats had revived Blaine's original plans for an inter-American meeting, and Cleveland issued the invitations, though fittingly Blaine convened the Washington meeting in October 1889. He was eager to attack British domination of Latin American markets by persuading the conferees to establish a customs union that set common tariffs against outsiders and lower, preferential duties within the union. Enthusiastic support for the idea came from important sectors of American manufacturing, agriculture, and shipping, some of whose leaders served as members of the U.S. delegation. Aside from his commercial objectives, Blaine also hoped the conference would produce machinery for arbitrating armed conflicts among hemispheric states. While achieving the admirable object of abolishing war in the hemisphere, arbitration would also reduce occasions for European intervention.

Blaine first arranged a whirlwind tour through major industrial cities that would advertise U.S. products to the Latin visitors and publicize the conference among the people. The results of the meeting itself, however, came as a great letdown. Throughout, both Argentina and Chile were suspicious, aloof, and generally uncooperative; most of the other Latin American states did their share of foot-dragging, too. Attentive U.S. citizens grew impatient with so much talk to so little purpose. After several months' work the conference finally disbanded without establishing either a customs union or an arbitration apparatus. To stimulate trade, interested nations were encouraged to conclude reciprocal trade agreements with one another; in 1891–92 Blaine negotiated eight of these that showed promise, but the new Cleveland administration and the Democratic Congress of 1894 allowed the treaties to lapse before their effects could be tested. The Latin American governments failed to ratify lesser conference resolutions. Thus, aside from setting a precedent for later meetings (in 1901 a second met in Mexico City) and creating an information bureau (the future Pan American Union), the long-awaited conference came and went without significant accomplishments.

New Orleans, Valparaiso, and Honolulu: Crises in Three Cities

Any reputation for good-neighborliness gained through America's role in the recent conference largely evaporated after three stormy episodes that followed. The first arose in March 1891 after a New Orleans jury acquitted eleven Italians suspected of Mafia ties on charges of murdering the city's police superintendent. A local mob reacted to the jury's decision by tearing the prisoners from their cells and lynching them while the police looked the other way. The Italian government demanded redress and punishment of the offenders, but Blaine shunned any responsibility, since the federal system did not authorize him to act on a problem of local justice. When this was found inadequate, he delivered a bombastic lecture on American civics and, in effect, told the Italians to take it or leave it. Rome recalled its minister to the United States, Washington reciprocated, and in both countries foolish men talked of war. But Rome backed off on learning that only three of the victims retained Italian citizenship at the time of their deaths. Harrison inserted a tacit apology in his annual message, and Blaine quietly sent $25,000 to the bereaved Italian families, using the state department's secret service fund and thus avoiding a request for monies from Congress. The incident became a memory—but in many countries the recollection was not flattering to the United States.

Adding to Uncle Sam's saber-rattling image and giving Americans their first war scare since the *Virginius* affair was the crisis with Chile, sparked by an incident in Valparaiso in October 1891. More than a hundred American sailors on shore leave from the USS *Baltimore*, many of them intoxicated, were suddenly attacked by local residents. Two sailors were killed, seventeen badly hurt, and many others beaten while Valparaiso police, even worse than their counterparts in New Orleans, joined in the assault before putting most of the Americans in jail to dry out. Perhaps drunken tars could expect no better treatment, although one U.S. officer flatly declared that the Americans were "properly drunk; they went ashore, many of them, for the purpose of getting drunk, which they did on Chilean rum paid for with good United States money. When in this condition they were more entitled to protection than if they had been sober. . . . Instead of protecting them, the Chileans foully murdered these men. . . ." (Three years later in Korea marines from the same *Baltimore* acted so badly an American diplomat lamented: "They get beastly drunk and carouse about the streets in a most disgraceful manner, frightening and surprising the Japs and Koreans.")

Because both sides got their backs up, the Valparaiso brawl nearly led to war. Relations between the two nations had been poor as long ago as 1865 when the United States turned its back while Spain was harassing its onetime colony. Chile in 1891 needed no reminder that Harrison's secretary of state was the same "Jingo Jim" Blaine who had tried to strip away her territorial gains from the War of the Pacific. More recent, and aggravating, was the American role in the revolution, just concluded a few weeks before the Valparaiso riot, in which the "Congressionalists" had defeated the incumbent, President Balmaceda. The United States had made several cardinal errors—appearing to support the unprogressive cause of the executive against a parliamentary claim to power; ineptly offering to mediate just as the rebels began to win; attempting to seize a rebel ship employed on legal business (according to a later U.S. court decision) of shipping arms bought in the United States to Chile; and granting asylum in the U.S. legation to some of the losers (Balmaceda died by his own hand in the Argentine legation, one of many besides the American to offer sanctuary). The worst error, needless to say, had been to back the loser. When the new president took office, Washington's minister boycotted the ceremony. President Harrison grumbled that Chile was ignorant of "how to use victory with dignity and moderation." Deliberately delaying recognition of the new regime, he added that "sometime it may be necessary to instruct them."

Why so much hostility? Wounded pride on both sides, of course. Furthermore, Chile's stiff-necked independence grated on American nerves more than in the past because of the ties between the victorious Congressionalists—especially Chile's navy—and Great Britain, seen as a threat to vital U.S. interests all over the hemisphere. The British presence in Chile was overwhelming, an American wrote in 1888; given England's domination of trade and Valparaiso's reliance on the English language and the pound sterling, the city was "nothing more than an English colony." With both Chile and the United States acting like rejected lovers, the Valparaiso affair spiraled into an emotional crisis. Still getting organized after the revolution, the Chileans were slow to act decently toward the victimized sailors. Their first responses to Washington's protests were studiously unrepentant, and Harrison threatened retaliation in his annual message of December 9, 1891 (the same in which he mollified the ruffled Italians). This in turn led to gratuitous insults of Harrison and his administration by the Chilean foreign minister, and the Americans howled for reprisal. Chile again raised temperatures January 20, 1982, when it denounced the U.S. minister and demanded his recall from Valparaiso. This was simply too much for Harrison, who sent an ultimatum on January 21st, threatening to break diplomatic relations unless Chile apologized immediately and made amends. Finally realizing their danger, Chile's government framed a conciliatory reply, which Washington received on January 26, a day after the impatient Harrison sent Congress a tacit bid to declare war. This time, it seems quite clear, Harrison was not bluffing, so Chile acted just in time. Its message was an abject apology and promise of indemnity for the injured seamen and families of the dead (later set at $75,000). Harrison grimly accepted.

Blaine, his zest for combat dead with the three children he had lost within a year, lay ill during the crisis. A few times he barely dragged himself to the White House to urge calm. Tracy's navy, its yards bustling with ominous activity, thirsted for conflict and solemnly debated the relative advantages of attacking Iquique or Lota. The president remained in charge throughout, drafting the correspondence and ultimatums. At the root of his pugnacity was a hypersensitive patriotism and a war veteran's insistence on avenging insults to the American uniform. Though these were Harrison's personal motives, his conduct of the affair reflected the spirit of the New Paradigm. Historians have shown that Britain acted with perfect neutrality throughout, but Washington saw dangers of foreign intrusion everywhere in the hemisphere. Chile was a long distance from the United States, but events in faraway countries (even internal politics) now seemed vitally important. Brandishing armed force had become an acceptable weapon of American diplomacy. However "modern" Washington's behavior, its results included a deeper embitterment of Chile toward the United States, a blow against the brotherly spirit of the Pan-American conference, a growing suspicion of Yankee diplomacy in other Latin American capitals, and—at home—a vigorous stoking of the fires of nationalism.

The sudden attempt to annex Hawaii in 1893 was the Harrison administration's final and most important diploma-

tic venture. With the Bering Sea controversy stilled in the
north and the Samoan question on hold in the south, the
stage was set to complete America's Pacific picket line with
an outpost in Hawaii. Along with Pago Pago in Samoa, Pearl
Harbor would give the United States two of the three finest
harbors in the Pacific (the third being Manila). The influence
of stateside settlers had continued growing since renewal of
the reciprocal trade treaty in 1887, but a new mainland duty
on Hawaiian sugar (mostly grown by Americans) in 1890
dealt a heavy blow to the economy. Aware that annexation
would bring them directly inside the U.S. tariff wall—as well
as abolish Hawaii's contract-labor system—the Americans
and their European-born allies found annexation to the
United States increasingly desirable and began pushing their
views aggressively. The young Queen Liliuokalani responded
by reasserting her own prerogatives and the primacy of
Hawaiian interests. Angered, the Americans decided to over-
throw her, proclaim a republic, and seek immediate annexation. But they needed help. It came from the expansionist
U.S. minister John L. Stevens, whose intervention in
January 1893 surpassed their wildest hopes. Acting on his
own authority, Stevens swiftly promised military support to
Liliuokalani's rebellious subjects, ordered 150 marines from
the offshore USS *Boston* to guard locations in Honolulu the
rebels had to control to succeed in their *coup*, and stood by
complacently while the rebels deposed the queen. The revo-
lutionaries then proclaimed a republic, which Stevens recognized even before Liliuokalani's main defense forces had a
chance to surrender. He also declared an American protectorate over Hawaii and raised the U.S. flag over Honolulu.
Approving everything else, Washington disavowed only the
protectorate, and that in language so ambiguous that Stevens
probably missed the disavowal. The stars and stripes did not
come down, and in Washington Secretary of State John W.
Foster and a party from Hawaii's provisional government
(which, incidentally, included no Hawaiians) soon sat across

a table to discuss terms. They finished their work February 14, and President Harrison, though lukewarm to the idea, sent the annexation treaty to the Senate on the fifteenth, only thirty days after Stevens had called out the marines and started the ball rolling.

The Senate, however, slowed down proceedings because of its own doubts and President-elect Cleveland's request for delay. Cleveland smelled a rat, or at least a thickening plot. Always suspicious of Republican diplomacy, he ordered former Democratic congressman James H. Blount of Georgia to investigate Stevens's shenanigans. Blount returned the marines to their ship, lowered the American flag, and reported to Cleveland that the revolution would never have come off without the minister's illicit meddling. Cleveland first tried to restore Queen "Lil" to her throne. Finding that both impractical and unpopular, he dropped the whole matter in the lap of Congress, which did nothing.

Despite its inconclusive outcome, the Hawaiian affair was significant in several respects. It sparked an important public debate that accentuated (and exaggerated) the gap between Cleveland and the Republicans, who now became more consciously expansionist than ever. The incident displayed facets of both old and new diplomatic paradigms. In traditional fashion, American initiative originated in Honolulu rather than Washington. Stevens's only "imperialist" orders were to secure U.S. cable-landing rights in Hawaii; his free hand resulted largely from the absence of cable ties to the mainland. The brisk way in which the Harrison administration pounced on its sudden opportunity, however, was a sign of new times. Its bold action responded to the dictates of "policy": concern about British and Japanese influence in Hawaii (though no foreign power raised objections to U.S. annexation), interest in reaping important economic advantages for the United States, and belief that holding Hawaii would protect American shipping lanes to Asia and guard an isthmian canal from dangers arising in the

Pacific. Backing administration reasoning throughout was a report from a new-era institution, the fledgling Office of Naval Intelligence.

GROVER CLEVELAND

Cleveland's handling of Hawaii epitomizes his approach to foreign policy. He was an unbending foe of annexing new territory, partly because he feared that imperialism would lead to an overbearing federal government. Nor was he attracted by the idea of bringing dark-skinned Polynesians into the republic. Stevens's behavior aroused his moral scruples. Though capable of squeezing partisan nectar from the plum of foreign policy, this mountainous man could withstand great popular pressure without flinching. He could also act clumsily and even irresponsibly, as witnessed by his chronic invitations to Congress to make the next move toward goals he refused to define. The return to power of this staunch traditionalist, however, did not signal a retreat to the Old Paradigm, as his policy in Hawaii itself makes clear. Like so many of his countrymen, Cleveland had arrived at a different view of foreign affairs since his first term in the eighties. Thus he opposed Hawaiian annexation, ever mindful of its Republican parentage, but was assiduous in maintaining America's special position in the islands.

Although the United States remained aloof from European matters, Cleveland tentatively raised the stakes in East Asia. Secretary of State Walter Q. Gresham declared that the Sino-Japanese War of 1894–95 was nothing for Americans to trouble themselves about, but Washington did not ignore this debut of Japanese power. Officials worried that a wounded China would be easy prey for rapacious imperialists, shutting the United States out of future opportunities. When Cleveland sent eight ships to Chinese waters, however, it was for the protection of U.S. citizens, mainly missionaries. Marines landed in both China and Korea on

[handwritten note: Week in Asia]

similar assignments. Otherwise the U.S. response to this war was confused. Jeffrey M. Dorwart writes that "Poor communications, Gresham's inexperience, and ignorance of actual conditions" forced the state department to rely on its ministers in the Far East, some of whom angled to enlist the United States on China's side, not what Washington wanted. Insofar as the American public registered an opinion, it was pro-Japanese. Besides, Cleveland and Gresham, who turned aside British proposals for cooperation in keeping Chinese ports open, wished to minimize U.S. involvement. Eventually, Washington escaped unscathed but without having helped much in ending the war. The Far Eastern piece in the New Paradigm mosaic was not yet firmly in place.

In Latin America Cleveland's second-term diplomacy became progressively more deliberate, aggressive, and expansionist. Walter LaFeber believes this was a thrust of "depression diplomacy," a concerted effort to pull the United States out of the slough of depression through a determined campaign to expand exports. Most other historians regard Cleveland's actions as politically motivated, an attempt from the autumn of 1893 onward to shed a timid reputation in foreign affairs. Both views are too narrow. Many factors were at work, including all the elements of the New Paradigm. Although Cleveland's Latin American "policy" took form through responses to a series of discrete incidents, the goal was clear enough: to stave off European threats to the political and economic influence of the United States in the Caribbean and along the northern shores of South America.

[handwritten margin note: New P. practice]

Minor Crises in the Hemisphere

Three examples of Cleveland's dealings with Latin America deserve mention. The first was his involvement in Brazil's civil war in 1893. Against the advice of its minister in Rio de Janeiro, Harrison's government had been the first to recognize the new Brazilian republic in 1890. The contest three years later pitted this new regime against rebels falsely rumored to back a return to monarchy. American officials also suspected that the rebels were getting aid and moral support from European countries, especially the ever-treacherous Britain, though London was actually so detached it still sent its Rio minister some of his instructions by mail. Most historians now credit Secretary Gresham with realizing the puniness of any European threat, yet he did tell the U.S. minister in Brazil "that it was time to take a stand on the Monroe Doctrine and let European nations generally know that we would maintain it even at the deplorable cost of a war." Uppermost in Gresham's mind was to go by the book in responding to a foreign insurgency. Though it was not eager to interfere, Washington bolstered the government by rejecting rebel requests to recognize their belligerency and honor their proclaimed blockade of Rio, which was aimed at choking off the government's supplies and customs revenues. To reinforce the right of American goods to enter the harbor, the United States sent down the largest foreign fleet present. Its armed escorts of merchant vessels, including one in which the American commander fired into the side of an obstructive rebel ship, effectively broke the blockade. The rebellion eventually petered out, but only in part thanks to Washington's actions. If newspapers' chortling about a struggle between "a whale and an elephant" are indicative, the American public did not take the affair very seriously; nor, apparently, did Cleveland and his advisers. The incident's significance lies in the new readiness of policymakers to go beyond strong words in defending the hemispheric interests of the United States.

In 1894, this time in Central America the United States became mildly entangled after Nicaragua moved to take control of the Miskito Indian reservation, technically a British ward for a third of a century. The picture of Queen Victoria protecting Central American aborigines was the sort of thing her countrymen could get quite solemn about, and Britain quickly dispatched soldiers to disarm the upstart Nicaraguans. Walter LaFeber has suggested that the quickening interest in commerce and an isthmian canal produced a crisis atmosphere in Washington. Yet no Anglo-American crisis occurred: the British contentedly departed from the scene once the Americans gave assurances that the Indians' rights would not be abused. Nicaragua formally absorbed the territory in December, about the time of another contretemps in British-Nicaraguan relations—the Corinto Affair. This trivial episode gets its name from the port occupied by the British after Nicaragua had arrested and deported one of their consular officers. It is important only for the jingoism it provoked in the United States. England demanded an apology and indemnity. Panic-stricken, Managua appealed to the United States for help, crying, please, uphold Señor Monroe's Doctrine! Cleveland and Gresham did nothing, however, believing neither that the doctrine was involved nor the British wrong in punishing the Nicaraguans. The queen's forces were gone by the spring of 1895. Long into that summer, however, Americans could be heard condemning Cleveland for his inaction.

The Venezuela Crisis

The Venezuela crisis of 1895–96 has always been something of a puzzle to students of Cleveland's second presidency. The bone of contention was the fifty-year-old dispute over the boundary between Venezuela and British Guiana. Implicated in the conflict were hundreds of thousands of acres of land (and a sizable population), the mouth of the Orinoco River with its potential for tapping trade with the interior of South America, and gold fields where the largest gold nugget in the world had recently been found. For many years Venezuela had asked for arbitration of the dispute, only to be refused by a haughty Britain, in no mood to do anything that would compromise the status of other British colonial boundaries. On three occasions since 1887 Cleveland had supported Venezuela's proposal for arbitration. The American public, however, remained generally unaware of the dispute until Congress passed resolutions in favor of arbitration in the early months of 1895 and the press picked up the scent. By mid-summer a diplomatic donnybrook seemed imminent.

Deciding to press the issue, Cleveland set Secretary Gresham to work composing a message to London. But the mild-mannered Gresham suddenly died, leaving the task to his successor, Richard Olney, a stern Bostonian who as attorney general had just put Eugene Debs in prison after the Pullman Boycott. (Years earlier Olney had banished his own daughter from the family home.) A newcomer to diplomacy, untrammeled by loyalties to old practices, he was alert to a system of issues, worrying about the harm his note might have on relations with Britain in the Far East. Cleveland, who insisted on highlighting the Monroe Doctrine to ensure moral grounds for any war that might result, closely scrutinized Olney's every word. After a few presidential inserts and deletions, the message was dispatched to Britain on July 20, 1895. It was an amazing document. Not only did Olney resort to harsh language in demanding international arbitration of the boundary line, but he backed his argument with variations on the Monroe Doctrine that must have sent the fifth president spinning in his grave. "Today," he asserted in the most notorious passage, "the United States is practically sovereign on this continent, and its fiat is law upon the subjects to which it confines its interposition . . . because, in addition to all other grounds, its infinite resources combined with its isolated position render it master of the situation and practically invulnerable as against any or all other powers."

Cleveland hoped for Britain's reply in time for his annual December message, and Olney had instructed his ambassador in London to use the cable "freely," but owing to bureaucratic blunders and an utter insensitivity to Washington's mood, the response of Prime Minister Salisbury (doubling as his own foreign minister) was exasperatingly slow to arrive. Thus, Cleveland's December 2 message merely recounted recent events in a blatantly anti-British account of the dispute, while affirming again the U.S. insistence on arbitration. Five days later the state department received Salisbury's reply. His arrogance a worthy match for Olney's belligerence, his manner that of a schoolmaster explaining simple ideas to small children, Salisbury refuted Olney's version of the Monroe Doctrine, denied its legal standing or relevance to the case at hand, heaped contempt on the Venezuelans, and peremptorily rejected the demand for arbitration. Cleveland, in his own words now "mad clean through," replied on December 17, 1895, in a message that ranks as one of the greatest bombshells ever tossed into the halls of Congress. In defiant tones he requested authorization to appoint his own commission to determine the correct boundary lines, stipulating that it was America's "duty . . . to resist by every means in its power as a willful aggression upon its rights and interests the appropriation by Great Britain of any lands or the exercise of governmental jurisdication over any territory which after investigation we have determined of right belongs to Venezuela." The normally phlegmatic president then assured the world that he was "fully alive to the responsibility incurred, and . . . all the consequences that may follow."

Cleveland's bombshell ignited an explosion of patriotism and Anglophobia. Congress immediately granted the requested authority. Dovish criticism of Cleveland's action and a brief Wall Street panic (caused mainly by Britishers unloading American securities) were overwhelmed by frenzied talk of war—a preview of the hysteria that would mark the Cuban crisis twenty-seven months later. Yet President Cleveland may well have been bluffing. His message contained several neat loopholes, especially the commission itself, which could ponder and examine until the disputants were restored to reason. The only military alert occurred after the climax of the crisis, when naval squadrons were told to keep up steam in late January 1896. Lord Salisbury's cabinet, however, had to take Cleveland seriously, and most people in Britain were dismayed. Almost as soon as the first wave of excitement passed, another feeling swept through both countries that war between the two great English-speaking nations would be a tragedy and absurdity.

Then, as feelers toward negotiations were just getting under way, the German Kaiser on January 3, 1896, ominously telegraphed public congratulations to President Kruger of the Boer Republic for repelling the "Jameson Raid," staged from neighboring British territory. South Africa swept Venezuela from the headlines in London, and Britain's anger turned toward Berlin. Acutely aware of their diplomatic isolation in Europe, Britain suddenly realized the value of a friendly United States. Overruling Salisbury on the 11th of January, the British cabinet decided on negotiations, deflating the crisis as abruptly as it had swelled. Negotiators quickly came to terms once they had agreed which issues Britain would or would not submit to arbitration. The results were anticlimactic: a Venezuelan-British treaty of arbitration in 1897 and an award from the arbitrators in 1899 that supported British claims more than Venezuelan. By that time no one in the United States cared. Far greater events occupied the limelight. Besides, Cleveland had already made his point.

But what, in fact, was it? Why had the erstwhile mayor of Buffalo thrown the gauntlet at the feet of the Third Marquis of Salisbury? To gain political credit through a vigorous twist of the lion's tail? Perhaps. The final months of 1895 were certainly an opportune time for that game. Cleveland was besieged by enemies, mainly fellow Democrats, for his domestic policies, especially for halting the silver-purchase program and allowing J. P. Morgan's Anglo-American banking syndicate to reap large profits while vainly trying to shore up U.S. gold reserves. Irish voters accused him of being a limey-lover. Expansionists of both parties indicted him for spinelessness: he had lowered the flag over Hawaii, waved aside congressional entreaties to use U.S. influence to end the massacre of Armenians in Turkey, and watched complacently while Britain bullied Nicaragua at Corinto. Could he permit further crumbling of Democratic unity? Could he afford more diplomatic inactivity? Could he forfeit the popularity to be gained from a rousing burst of Anglophobia? As a Democrat from Texas wrote him: "Turn this Venezuela question up or down, North, South, East or West, and it is a 'winner.' "

Cleveland surely entertained such thoughts, but only with passing effect. He was neither a shrewd man, nor devious, nor cunning. He was unimaginative, and mulish, not likely to crumple under political pressure. Nearing the end of his second term, he was not considering a third. At any rate, he had no reason to believe that his actions on Venezuela could either reunite the Democrats or strengthen his own political position, for those who most loudly applauded a tough policy were either Republican imperialists or Democratic and Populist silverites who, seeing in Cleveland the devil incarnate, would effectively purge him from his party the following summer by slating William Jennings Bryan for president. Besides, had Cleveland been looking for political advantage, he would not have allowed Britain's delay in answering the Olney salvo to keep him from conducting the Anglophobe chorus in his annual message of December the 2d; instead, he waited until Salisbury's obnoxious response had arrived before sending to Congress the crisis-provoking message of the 17th.

If politics cannot explain Cleveland's actions, neither can morality. What he knew of the boundary controversy— and his information was both biased and incomplete— outraged his sense of fair play, but if fairness in a foreign land was his goal, why hadn't he taken up the cudgels for Venezuela in 1887? Or why not marshal American forces in response to the flagrant immorality of the Armenian massacres? Because (in answering the first question) the implications of British high-handedness in the hemisphere seemed far more disturbing in 1895 than in the eighties; and (in reply to the second) because events in faraway Turkey did not threaten U.S. interests. The keys for the president were Venezuela's proximity and his conviction that British policy there directly threatened American interests.

Cleveland acted on the basis of a distorted picture of the boundary dispute, drawn for him by Venezuelan lobbyists. However, he was not striking out at phantoms. British control of the Orinoco and the new gold fields might harm the U.S. economy in the future; more to the point, it could set off a general round of European poaching on American grounds. The idea was not fantastic in a golden age of European imperialism. The scramble for empire had intensified in the thirty-three months between Cleveland's inauguration in March 1893 and his bellicose message on Venezuela. In Asia, France had reduced Laos to a protectorate and joined Russia and Germany in forcing Japan to disgorge the mainland gains from her war with China. In Africa, Italy had come to terms with England on shares of East Africa and launched a campaign to conquer Ethiopia; Belgium was attempting to find territory on the Upper Nile; Germany had carved out the boundaries of the Cameroons in agreements with Britain and France, while the latter had taken over Guinea, the Ivory Coast, the Dahomey and begun the conquest of Madagascar; Britain had made a protectorate of Uganda, occupied Matabeleland, annexed Pondoland and Togoland, organized Rhodesia and the East African Protectorate, and annexed "British" Bechuanaland to her Cape Colony. As for the Western Hemisphere, Joseph Smith has shown that "the assumption of diplomatic conflict between the United States and Europe over Latin America was illusory," including in Venezuela. But the way Cleveland saw it, Germany and Britain had displayed an alarming interest in the Brazilian rebellion; France had seemed menacing while hectoring Santo Domingo with naval demonstrations and claiming Brazilian territory for French Guiana (which led to combat between French and Brazilian troops in May 1895); and Great Britain had not only been badgering Nicaragua, but had also occupied the islet of Trinidad despite the claims of Brazil.

What were Americans to think? What did the altered perspective of the New Paradigm suggest to them? Cleveland was not alone in thinking that insatiable European powers were taking dangerous liberties in the backyard of the United States. The president did not fret over the interests of Venezuela; never consulting her, Olney acted, in Gerald Eggert's words, "as if he held blank power-of-attorney for that country." What worried both men was the political, economic, and strategic threat being fashioned by outside powers. Cleveland was bent on quashing that threat and securing acknowledgement of U.S. supremacy in the hemisphere. This grim determination, which replaced the vague uneasiness of 1887, reflected changes in both landscape and perspective: the European imperialist impulse had gained momentum, and Americans' view of their own country and others had changed. The United States was more powerful and yet more vulnerable than when Cleveland had first been president. The outside world had more bearing on American welfare than before, thus making "policies" essential. Cleveland was not yet prepared, as Theodore Roosevelt was in 1904, to lay down a general rule for future relations among the United States, Latin America, and Europe, but he knew what he was doing—asserting the supremacy of the United States in the New World.

Cuba

This insistence on America's dominant role also appeared in Cleveland's approach to the new Cuban rebellion beginning in February 1895. The rebellion fed on most of the same grievances that had nourished the Cuban war of 1868–78. American investors had meanwhile taken over large sectors of the Cuban economy; by 1894, writes Louis A. Pérez, Jr., "the United States received almost 90 percent of Cuba's

Involvement

total exports and . . . provided 40 percent of its imports
. . . ." Americans were among the interested parties when
Congress in 1894 slapped a 40 percent duty on Cuban sugar
imports (in the same act that lowered duties on Hawaiian
sugar). A severe depression settled on Cuba, fertilizing the
ground for an uprising that quickly grew to a full-scale revolution. Early in 1896 Spain turned over command of its armies to General Valeriano Weyler, known as "the Butcher"
for his tactics in the seventies, who now swept peasants into
"reconcentration" camps to remove them as recruits or
suppliers for the rebel armies. Hunger and disease struck the
camps and thousands died. With equal dedication to the
compounding of misery, the insurgents sought to paralyze
the economy through a scorched-earth strategy, fully aware
that many plantations and sugar mills put to the torch were
owned by American citizens who might demand protection
from their government, thus provoking U.S. intervention.
Working for the rebels in the United States was the Cuban
Junta, a large body of exiles, naturalized U.S. citizens of
Cuban birth, and native American sympathizers. The Junta
raised money, distributed propaganda, lobbied in Washington, and smuggled soldiers and ammunition into Cuba.
Editors discovered a ready audience for sensational Cuban
news. The American public, still on pins and needles from
the Venezuela crisis, anxiously awaited Washington's reaction to events in Cuba. Certainly something had to be done!
America could not tolerate such barbarities and bloodshed
just ninety miles from its shores!

José Martí, the Cuban patriot, had earlier remarked:
"Once the United States is in Cuba, who will get her out?"
Cleveland, who shared this concern, opposed annexing Cuba
and thus hoped to prevent armed intervention. He came
close to intervention, nonetheless, as he moved warily from
a neutrality weighted in sympathy toward Spain, to an offer of mediation biased in favor of the rebels, and finally to
solemn warnings that an impatient America might have to
intervene in defense of its own interests. The first position,

Transformation

lasting till the spring of 1896, dated from the 1895 proclamation of neutrality, which was accompanied by recognition of the rebels' insurgency (but not belligerency). Though U.S. neutrality laws were difficult to enforce, the administration did as well as could be expected, sharply warning Americans not to engage in prorebel activities in the United States. Although Cleveland and Olney grew concerned about damage to American interests in Cuba, at this stage they accepted Madrid's claim that the insurrection would soon die out, supported as it was only by the dregs of Cuban society. The administration even encouraged Spain in a friendly way to hurry up the campaign of suppression. Cleveland and Olney began to worry, however, that a breakdown of Spanish authority would invite a European takeover or that Cuban independence itself might lead to chaos. Whether they knew it or not, their fears encompassed the seeds of intervention.

Congress announced its preferences in the spring of 1896 by passing a concurrent resolution recognizing Cuba's belligerency and urging the president to extract Cuban independence from Spain. Cleveland ignored the resolution but moved in its direction, partly because of pressure but also owing to his own revised estimate of the rebellion. He now adopted Hamilton Fish's old policy—urging Spain to end the rebellion through wholesale concessions. Though still unwilling to recognize their belligerency, Washington was rapidly concluding that Spain could not put down the rebels forcibly. American policy was in flux, as Cleveland, swallowing his distaste for annexation, also hinted at the idea of buying the island and sounded out London about possible American annexation (to which the British replied: "It's no affair of ours."). These gestures, however, were only branch lines off the main track of state department diplomacy. In April 1896, Olney counseled Spain to make major reforms throughout the island, which he promised the United States would encourage the Cubans to accept. His message declared American interest in spurring the development of "free" governments in the hemisphere; ending the suffering and tragedies of war; restoring trade with Cuba, reduced since 1894 by half its normal volume of $100 million annually; and halting the destruction of American investments, then worth about $40 million. Olney also told Spain that armed U.S. intervention was a possibility as long as violence continued in Cuba. Besides the ideological, humanitarian, and economic objectives cited by Olney, the administration also was anxious to safeguard prospects for an isthmian canal and to prevent Spain from summoning European aid in defeating the rebels. The McKinley administration would find little to add to this rationale of 1896.

Spain rejected Olney's bid and, now suspicious of U.S. intentions, tried to put together a coalition of European powers to set against American pressure. But when Hannis Taylor, U.S. minister in Madrid, got wind of this project and protested, it died aborning. Spanish-American relations deteriorated rapidly as the sands of time ran out on Cleveland's government. In his last annual message, on December 7, 1896, the president went a step further, citing the damage being done to American interests, described as "by no means of a wholly sentimental or philanthropic character." Not disguising his disbelief in Spain's ability to quell the rebellion, he advocated granting Cuban autonomy within the Spanish empire. Although still holding back on recognizing either Cuban belligerency or independence, he warned Spain (and repeated the warning in February) that if the "senseless slaughter" and destruction continued, Americans would have no choice but direct intervention. The United States, he declared, "is not a nation to which peace is a necessity."

But he would walk no closer to the brink, as he demonstrated late in December 1896 when he ordered Olney to denounce a resolution to recognize Cuban independence then making its way through Congress. Olney pronounced recognition an executive responsibility, vowing complete disregard of the measure should it pass. The Capitol Hill initiative collapsed. Cleveland's obstinacy at this juncture had several sources. First, he remained unconvinced that the Cubans deserved belligerent status, which in any case could free Spain from her duty to protect American property in Cuba. Recognition of Cuban independence he deemed even less warranted, likely to provoke Spain to a declaration of war, and tantamount to accusing Spain of violating the Monroe Doctrine. This in turn would compel American action—that is, war, which he believed would lead willy-nilly to annexation. Finally, Cleveland shrank from doing anything that would tie the hands of the new president without giving him a chance to make his own choices. The Spanish-American War turned out to be McKinley's war, not because Cleveland was an old-fashioned isolationist with a stiffer backbone than his successor, but because he left office just in time.

FIVE

War, Policy, and Imperialism at the End of the Century, 1897–1900

William McKinley was elected president in 1896 on a platform calling for a strong navy, a stout Monroe Doctrine, "the eventual withdrawal of the European powers from this hemisphere," independence for Cuba, control over Hawaii, purchase of the Virgin Islands, and "the ultimate union of all

English-speaking parts of the continent by the free consent of its inhabitants." Hovering over the new president's shoulder was a clique of eager imperialists: Assistant Secretary of the Navy Theodore Roosevelt, Captain Alfred T. Mahan, Senators Henry Cabot Lodge and Cushman K. Davis, writer Brooks Adams, and others. They were determined to implement what Lodge termed "the large policy," which, according to historian Julius W. Pratt, was aimed at making the United States "the indisputably dominant power in the western hemisphere, possessed of a great navy, owning and controlling an Isthmian canal, holding naval bases in the Caribbean and the Pacific, and contesting, on at least even terms with the greatest powers, the naval and commercial supremacy of the Pacific Ocean and the Far East." McKinley, Pratt wrote, was "clay in the hands of the little group of men who knew all too well what use to make of war."

At least this is how the story once began, but few historians still accept the tale of an imperialist cabal and a hysterical people pushing a rudderless McKinley against his will into war. The more recent assessment of McKinley parallels the revised view of the nineties presented in this book. Most of the "clique" just mentioned stood on the margins of power in 1897–98; they exercised less influence than such businesslike and moderate senators as William B. Allison, Stephen B. Elkins, Orville H. Platt, and John C. Spooner; quiet loyalists like William R. Day (at first assistant secretary of state, then secretary), not noisy warriors and colonialists, had the president's ear. McKinley himself was far abler than most people realized. This Civil War major and longtime Ohio politican cannot be called either brilliant or imaginative, but he was intelligent, unruffled by crisis, and effective in getting his own way. Historians have always found it hard to get a fix on McKinley, a result of his reticence, his oblique way of doing things, and his aversion to putting anything important on paper, a habit reinforced when he discovered an ally in the telephone. However hard to pin down, he is now known as a resourceful political leader and minor master in managing those around him. This hardworking and demure Methodist, outshadowed in reputation by the gaudy Teddy Roosevelt, paved the way to the modern presidency, as the studies of Lewis L. Gould and Robert C. Hilderbrand have shown. He provided the lead for Congress and the people in foreign affairs, traveling through the nation to mobilize support for his objectives. He deftly ruled his own cabinet. He appealed to the new worship of scientists and professionals by using them to clothe his policies with respectability. In war he did not flinch at managing the news or acting in the darkness of secrecy. When he deemed it necessary, he took far-reaching steps without asking Congress for approval. He could not do all this alone: the White House staff grew from six to eighteen people in his first nine months in office and numbered more than eighty by 1901. McKinley, in short, needed no cabal to tell him what to do. He was certain that the United States should play a greater role in world affairs, to protect its wider interests, to gain "American supremacy in world markets," and to do good.

WAR AND EMPIRE

McKinley wanted peace but from the outset of his administration was prepared to use force in Cuba as a last resort. Stewart L. Woodford, his minister in Madrid, reported in September 1897 that Spain had no Cuban "policy." But McKinley did. The president mapped his course cautiously, hoping to avoid a war that would damage the advancing business recovery and spawn other problems, but within six months he had come closer to war than Cleveland ever had, and for two main reasons. First, while Cleveland had often disregarded the means Spain might use in putting down the rebellion, McKinley as early as June 26, 1897, demanded a speedy end to the "uncivilized and inhumane conduct" of the war. "Butcher" Weyler's strategy having by then caused

about 100,000 fatalities, the president called on Spain henceforth to fight "according to military codes of civilization."
Second, unlike his predecessor, McKinley indicated an aversion to imposing any settlement on the Cubans that they
found unacceptable. The combination of Spain's harsh coun-
terinsurgency tactics and the rebels' refusal to accept Cuban
autonomy as a solution meant that by the summer of 1897
Washington and Madrid were careening rapidly toward a
head-on collision—well before the "yellow" press campaign
for "Cuba Libre," the de Lôme letter, or the sinking of the
Maine.

Other issues, too, raised the odds in favor of war. The
rebellion caused uncertainty in American political and economic life and, the state department complained in July
1897, produced "a continuous irritation within our borders";
imposing peace on the island might become necessary to restore American "tranquillity." Patrolling the Gulf of Mexico
to enforce U.S. neutrality laws and keeping the navy on
alert cost money. Moreover, the longer the Cuban problem
remained unresolved the more likely some European power
might exploit Washington's distraction; thus in the winter of
1897 Germany made a belligerent gunboat demonstration
against Haiti, denounced the Monroe Doctrine, and announced plans to build new warships for the Caribbean and
South Atlantic. In faraway China, Germany seized Kiaochow in November, a disturbing portent about which the
United States could do nothing so long as Cuba monopolized
its attention.

In an August 1897 note, Madrid had shown little interest
in American concerns; in September and October McKinley
increased the pressure through the U.S. minister. Spain was
required to end the fighting (using humane tactics) and carry
out key reforms in Cuba, or the United States might reluctantly intervene. Woodford also warned Madrid against looking for support in other European capitals. With an eye to
hurrying events along and underlining the large U.S. stake in
Cuba, McKinley also offered his services as a mediator.

Under attack from European states and domestic critics as well, Spain now saw peril ahead unless it took decisive measures. A new ministry in late October promised to find a quick, yet humane end to the civil war, recalling Weyler as a sign of its serious intent. Though still rejecting mediation, in November Spain suspended the reconcentration policy, proclaimed a series of reforms, and issued a decree for Cuban "autonomy." On close examination, however, the autonomy scheme looked phony. Washington, growing skeptical of Spain's sincerity and its reforms' chances of success, began to prepare for action. As though nothing much had happened, McKinley in his annual message in December again pressed the case: reform Cuba from top to bottom or face American intervention.

As 1897 came to a close, McKinley received hopeful messages from Woodford in Madrid, urging him to give time for Spanish reforms to do their work. But the president was also poring over the reports of U.S. Consul Fitzhugh Lee, on the scene in Havana, who was convinced that neither repression nor autonomy would end the rebellion. With the new year, the pace toward war quickened. Lee told the state department that "Autonomy is not cutting any ice" and Woodford, now pessimistic, that Spain was stalling. On January 17, 1898, Queen Regent Maria implored Woodford to have faith in Spanish reforms and let up on the pressure. But massive riots by pro-army and antireform groups had erupted in Havana five days before her plea, setting off a wave of skepticism in Washington. Even if Spain were sincere (now doubted), even if the plans for autonomy were genuine (also doubted since they reserved final authority to Madrid), the Spanish government now seemed helpless to carry out its edicts against the will of Cuban loyalists and the army. McKinley nonetheless stuck to his familiar policy road, though no one can say with certainty why. Perhaps it was because he never liked leading decisively until he knew his followers were all in position. In the judgment of Louis A. Pérez, he may have been playing a deep game aimed at getting Spain to turn control of Cuba over to the United States before the rebels seized the island for themselves in an out-and-out military victory. Or, more likely, he may still have hoped to avoid war, however bleak his prospects of succeeding. That he now sided with the pessimists, however, sent waves across the Atlantic, where Spain intensified its bid for big-power support and otherwise adopted a strategy of delay—the proverbial mañanaism.

Two blows rocked Spanish-American relations in February. First, a private letter of Spain's minister in Washington, Enrique Dupuy de Lôme, was intercepted by a Junta member and published in a New York newspaper on February 9. De Lôme's most shocking phrase, calling McKinley "weak and a bidder for the admiration of the crowd," was bad enough, prompting the hapless diplomat to ask for his passport before McKinley could demand his ouster. More serious than de Lôme's insults, however, were his hints that neither the Cuban reforms nor current trade talks were being carried out in good faith. Spain compounded its sin by apologizing belatedly and begrudgingly. Washington's doubts that Spain could actually revamp Cuba were now joined by a belief that she would not even try. Former critics of the administration, red-faced from Spanish duplicity, urged McKinley to do whatever was necessary to end the war in Cuba. The president himself, perhaps eager to build more pressure to which he could then respond, released Lee's reports on the failure of Cuban pacification.

Six days after de Lôme's letter appeared, the second-class battleship *Maine*, sent out on a mission combining vigilance and goodwill after Havana's January riots, exploded and sank in the city's harbor, killing 260 American seamen. Headlines and mass meetings screamed for vengeance. Anger at McKinley's Buddhalike patience mounted in Congress. Although the disaster probably resulted from an internal explosion, sparked by a coal-bunker fire—or even from insurgent sabotage—it almost certainly did not result from Spanish treachery. Madrid could only lose from the catastrophe, as quickly became clear, for this event probably made war unavoidable if not determined its exact timing. McKinley's first reaction, however, was to order a naval inquiry and refrain from any recriminations. "The country can afford to withhold its judgment," he said, "and not strike an avenging blow until the truth is known." Although McKinley would now begin quietly preparing for war, he refused to be stampeded into it by the popular frenzy. Hostilities would not start until the *Maine* had lain at the bottom of Havana harbor for more than two months.

But time was running out. The United States informally warned de Lôme's successor in the first week of March that the day of reckoning was rapidly nearing unless Spain quickly met American demands. McKinley simultaneously asked Congress for $50 million (a serious sum in 1898) to get ready for war; Congress complied at once, deeply impressing Spanish leaders but stiffening the will of Cuban insurgents. On March 17 Senator Redfield Proctor of Vermont, an unflappable moderate just back from a Cuban tour, made a speech that electrified the country with its pictures of Spanish cruelties and failed reforms. Proctor's call for intervention gained greater significance because of rumors that McKinley had sent him to Cuba and even cleared his speech. A few days later, the naval board of inquiry informed McKinley that the *Maine* was sunk by an external explosion, thus ruling out an on-board accident. McKinley buried the report for a week, maybe in hopes that the threat of disclosure would force Spain to accept his terms.

These terms were misinterpreted by historians arguing that McKinley caved in to jingoes even though Spain at the last moment buckled to all his demands. But she did not. McKinley's "final" terms were sent to Spain on March 27, 1898, after he had already promised to submit the entire Cuban matter to Congress by April 15 unless Madrid in the meantime responded as desired. The demands were hard: Spain must declare an immediate armistice to last until October 1, abolish the reconcentration policy for good, carry out thorough war-relief measures, and permit the president to mediate the conflict if a settlement with the rebels could not be reached during the armistice. The last item was McKinley's trump card since it encompassed an implicit demand for Cuban independence should he decide on it in the role of mediator. The wording of this item was opaque, perhaps as Lewis Gould suggests because McKinley worried that clearer language would provoke an automatic rejection. Woodford, now returned to his hopeful mood, then presented the demand so circumspectly that Madrid probably missed his meaning. In any case, Spain avoided the crucial issue of Cuban independence in her reply.

That reply, made March 31, 1898, promised fundamental reforms (how many times had Americans heard this in the past thirty years?) and what looked like a firm promise to end reconcentration. Spain also offered an armistice if the rebels asked for it. Because this suspiciously resembled an invitation to the rebels to lay down their weapons, and because Spain had also rejected mediation, McKinley felt he had to proceed with his "war" message. But not at once, for he still seemed to hope for peace. Justifying the delay to allow time for Americans to evacuate Cuba, McKinley cannily massaged half a dozen different leaders and groups in a ten-day effort to prevent war. While marking time, he listened politely on April 7 as a delegation of European diplomats relayed their nations' hopes for peace, a *pro forma* affair of little concern since McKinley knew that neither Germany nor Britain would risk American displeasure over the issue. According to John L. Offner, he may himself have engineered this bit of theater as a device to calm public opinion. Finally, just as the president decided to go ahead with his message, news arrived that Spain had made a new concession, unilaterally announcing an armistice but leaving its duration up to the judgment of the Spanish commander in Cuba. Woodford was gulled by this concession, but not McKinley. When Assistant Secretary of State Day asked the Spanish minister whether anything in this last cable might be construed to mean a commitment to Cuban independence, the answer was negative: no Spanish government could give up Cuba and survive another day in office. McKinley did not want war—he wanted Spain to surrender, and she wouldn't.

Thus, after nearly three years of maneuvering, Spain and the United States had reached a dead end. McKinley finally sent his message to Congress on April 11. Like most presidents going to war, he threw in everything but the kitchen sink in a statement of grievances. Then he asked for authority to end the Cuban rebellion in terms that intriguingly suggested he may have contemplated a "third-force" intervention—restraining both warring parties while preserving maximum freedom of action in deciding the future of Cuba. As an afterthought, he added a paragraph calling attention to Spain's recent armistice proclamation. For several days Congress tried to move McKinley to recognize the rebels as the government of Cuba, but the president wanted a free hand in dealing with the Cubans. Granting recognition would legally subject U.S. actions to the review of a Cuban government. Refusing recognition, on the other hand, a state department official noted on April 8, would offer a chance to "dictate the terms of peace and control the organization of an independent government in Cuba." In the end a majority in both houses of Congress fell in line against recognition— strong evidence that McKinley was commanding events and following a calculated line of policy at precisely the time historians traditionally described him as spinelessly submitting to congressional and public opinion. A joint war resolution emerged from Congress on April 19. Proclaiming the end of Spanish sovereignty in Cuba, it authorized McKinley to employ armed force to end the rebellion. The Teller Amendment promised that the United States would not annex Cuba, partly as a way of avoiding responsibility for the Cuban debt. By April 25, declarations and counterdeclarations had brought Spain and the United States into a state of official hostilities. Americans had entered their first foreign war in a half century.

Many of McKinley's contemporaries anticipated the

view of later historians that he was dragged into war against his will. Senator John C. Spooner believed that war was avoidable, "but the current was too strong, the demagogues too numerous, the fall elections too near." This interpretation cannot bear the weight of recent scholarship, though works as new as David F. Trask's comprehensive *The War with Spain in 1898* (1981) still adhere to it in modified form. Robert C. Hilderbrand's path-breaking study, *Power and the People: Executive Management of Public Opinion in Foreign Affairs, 1897–1921* (1981) argues more persuasively that the president worried less about the political consequences of defying public opinion than he did about working it to his own advantage. His staff did not even show him the apoplectic stories in the "yellow press," which they dismissed as "the products of degenerate minds" that "misrepresent[ed] public opinion." Though anxious about the directions of public sentiment, McKinley was probably content to have it drift toward war, resigned to the prospect that this would be the outcome of his diplomacy, however hard he tried to avoid it. The American people would be ready for war if it came, yet— should he come up with a peaceful settlement against all odds—not so emotionally aroused to ruin his work.

McKinley, of course, did not prefer war; few statesmen have said after the fighting, "I wanted war." But he did want what only war could provide—an end to violence in Cuba, which outraged his sense of decency, prolonged instability in the economy, smashed investment and trade with Cuba, created the spectacle of an America unable to master affairs close to home, threatened to incite a politically dangerous outburst of jingoism, and diverted policymakers' attention from historic events in China (as McKinley confidant Whitelaw Reid wrote, "as soon as Cuba is out of the way the present Chinese complications are likely to develope [*sic*] a great deal of interest for us"). Only if Spain had given in to all of McKinley's terms could he have prevented war, which was no more in the cards than it was for the president in this new era to abandon Cuba altogether. Neither spineless nor bellicose, he demanded what he thought morally irreproachable and essential to American interests. He did make errors. In trying both to coerce Spain and find a door through which she could exit from the Caribbean, he unwittingly backed himself into a corner. Every time he increased the pressure on Spain, he lost leverage over the Cuban insurgents. Finally, he failed to test the fit of the other fellow's shoes, not realizing Spain's passion for holding on to the Pearl of the Antilles in the face of hostile pressure. Spain's leaders, with their own moral and political imperatives, elected war over surrender.

The familiar story of the war itself belongs in military and naval histories. Spanish forces were no match for even the ill-prepared Americans, who captured Cuba and Puerto Rico, and, in the war's most dramatic event (other than Teddy Roosevelt's charge up San Juan Hill), Commodore George Dewey defeated the Spanish fleet at Manila on May 1, 1898. American naval movements feinted at an attack on Spain itself, prompting agreement to an armistice on August 12, 1898. The United States had suffered only 379 combat deaths in what John Hay called a "splendid little war."

During the war Spain received nothing from European governments but the thin gruel of sympathy. The French envoy to Washington, who described Americans as "ignorant, brutal, and quite capable of carelessly destroying the complicated European structure," arranged the armistice in August. Great Britain opened her arms to the new world nation, welcoming her into the ranks of the great imperial powers and smoothing her path in other ways as well. Even before the outset of war, London officials handed over intelligence about Spanish diplomacy in Europe to Ambassador John Hay. During the war itself, "neutral" Britain expelled a Spanish agent from Canada on dubious grounds yet winked at American espionage originating in Gibraltar, denied coal to a Spanish fleet off Egypt while finding it for American ships in several locations, expedited U.S. contacts with the exiled Filipino leader Emilio Aguinaldo, and allowed Dewey to send messages from the Philippines to

Washington over the Hong Kong cable. Spain complained to no avail.

The British also responded favorably to the American annexation of Hawaii, finally accomplished in 1898. This affair had been in limbo since Cleveland's repudiation of the 1893 treaty, and anti-imperialists hoped that McKinley, too, would turn a deaf ear to the annexationists. Instead, he sent a new treaty to the Senate in June 1897. Failing to attract the necessary two-thirds majority, the project stalled. War with Spain gave the administration new reasons to push for annexation and an urgency borne of fear that other powers might insist on *quid pro quos* in case the United States emerged from the war with a clutch of new possessions. This time McKinley sidestepped Senate ratification and requested annexation through a joint resolution, requiring only a simple majority in each house of Congress. All the old expansionist arguments resurfaced in debate: duty and glory, economic advantage, security for the west coast of the mainland, and the prevention of foreign incursions in a U.S. sphere of influence. External threats no longer seemed academic after 1897, when Japan clashed with Hawaii over its ban on Japanese immigration and protested Washington's new annexation treaty. Though the crisis quickly subsided, Captain Mahan had believed it raised a "very real present danger of war"; Washington had ordered U.S. naval commanders to seize Hawaii and proclaim a protectorate in case Japan resorted to force.

Dewey's *coup de main* at Manila stimulated further annexationist sentiment, adding to the list of motives. The United States was now deeply entangled in East Asian affairs; Hawaii, long coveted as a mid-Pacific bastion for the defense of the West Coast and a future isthmian canal, took on a new role as indispensable steppingstone to Asia. "To maintain our flag in the Philippines," declared the *New York Sun,* "we must raise our flag in Hawaii." After lengthy debate and vigorous lobbying by McKinley, the House approved the annexation resolution 290–91 in June and the

Senate 42–21 in July. The nuptials between the United States and Hawaii finally took place only after the lovely islands came to be desired not so much for themselves as their value in sustaining the new thrust into East Asia. Action that shortly before seemed optional appeared essential in the era of the New Paradigm.

The sudden flush of victory in war produced a flurry of imperialist proposals. Congress again resounded with the rhetoric of Davy Crockett spread-eaglism. America would expand from the frozen wastes of the Yukon to the frigid reaches of Cape Horn, gobbling up every island in the Caribbean. She would plunge into the contest for China. Interest in the Virgin Islands reappeared, especially after rumors in 1900 that Germany had its eyes on them. (Germany was indeed tempted, but not enough to risk offending the United States.) Many Americans were inspired by the thought of carrying the world's primitives into the modern age with Anglo-Saxon government, sanitary reform, the little red schoolhouse, and Yankee work habits. More prosaically, the U.S. Naval Board urged the government to retain the Philippines and acquire island bases in the Marianas, off the coasts of China and South America, and in the Caribbean.

The United States government had rather precise goals in mind. Some it achieved without regard to other powers, as when it annexed Hawaii in 1898 and occupied Wake Island (between Hawaii and Guam) early in 1899. But other objectives required negotiations with Spain in Paris, where peace talks began October 1, 1898. McKinley chose his delegates with cunning: the former secretary of state William R. Day, full of doubts about taking the Philippines but McKinley's man, much respected by his colleagues; Whitelaw Reid of the *New York Tribune*, a Republican luminary, 1892 vice-presidential candidate, and unabashed imperialist; and three senators who would ratify (and presumably defend) their own handiwork—William P. Frye and Cushman K. Davis, both Republican expansionists, and, in the name of bipartisanship, George Gray, a Democratic anti-imperialist. McKinley sent them off to Paris without telling them what to do with the Philippines. Soon after their arrival, Spain's ambassador to France entreated Reid: "Do not forget that we are poor; do not forget that we are vanquished; do not forget that after all it was Spain that discovered America; do not forget that this is the first great war you have had with a nation on the continent of Europe, or with any foreign nation; that you have had an astonishing victory, and that you cannot complete it without showing magnanimity."

But magnanimity was not much on the delegates' minds. Most of the wrangling at the conference centered on Cuba. McKinley, worried about the direction an insurgent-ruled Cuba might take, had distanced the United States from the rebels during the war, refusing them any part in the surrender of Spanish armies. Accepting the Teller Amendment's oath against annexation as a nuisance, the administration determined to "free" Cuba, afterward extracting from it the gist of control through a protectorate and control of Guantanamo Bay. Day, Reid, and company, therefore, turned aside Spain's proposal that the United States annex Cuba along with its $400 million debt, mostly incurred in the war against the rebels. They did, however, demand the cession of Puerto Rico, and—responding to clamorous commodores—the island of Guam in the Marianas. The most vital issue at the conference was the fate of the Philippines—more than seven thousand islands and seven million people. After a Hamletlike pause, McKinley demanded these, too: their sovereignty was transferred to the United States in return for a face-saving payment of $20 million to Spain. The delegates from both nations signed the completed treaty on December 10, 1898.

For many years historians pictured the annexation of the Philippines as a kind of quirk, acquiesced in by a president who scarcely knew where they were. While it is certainly true that only war with Spain produced the annexation of the Philippines, they did not drop out of the blue into a dumbfounded McKinley's lap. Influential Americans knew perfectly well the location of the Philippines; they also knew of Aguinaldo's armed rising against Spain, if only through articles appearing in important magazines in 1896 and 1897. In 1895–96 navy officers had put together contingency plans for attacking the Philippines in case of war with Spain. McKinley, aware of these plans as early as September 1897, approved instructions for Dewey to prepare their execution.

With the beginning of the war, McKinley began making decisions that leaned heavily toward annexation. As soon as the guns cooled from Dewey's victory, McKinley could have declared it a tactical triumph and sent the commodore on his way. Instead, without consulting Congress or knowing the full extent of the victory, he immediately summoned volunteers for Philippines service and dispatched troops to occupy Manila. He first ordered 5,000 to go, upped this to more than 10,000 by the 11th of May, and had signed orders for more than 20,000 by the 29th of the month. Historian David Trask views these developments as war-shortening measures, an attempt by the president to strong-arm Spain to the conference table. Wanting a quick end to the war, however, was not inconsistent with getting poised to master new territories afterward. The first contingent of 11,000 men, almost double Dewey's original request, began arriving by the end of June and more soon followed. On August 13 (one day after the armistice) the troops seized Manila from the Spanish garrison; as in Cuba, American forces by express order refused to allow local rebels anywhere near the action. In Washington, such "large policy" imperialists as Mahan and Lodge briefly favored annexing only the harbor of Manila, leaving the rest to Spain. Soon, however, McKinley (who from the first may have intended taking more) and his advisers came to look on Manila as militarily indefensible without the rest of Luzon, and it was only another short step to conclude that defense of Luzon required holding the rest of the Philippines. Whitelaw Reid wrote to John Hay, October 16, 1898, "Have you considered that there is hardly one of those islands from which you cannot shoot across to another!" Even Aguinaldo remarked that going all the way was better than taking half steps, which would lead to "partition and a subsequent history similar to Poland's." Thus, the U.S. delegation in Paris received instructions to demand all the Philippines; annexing Luzon alone, McKinley asserted through his secretary of state, could "not be justified on political, commercial, or humanitarian grounds."

Exactly when McKinley decided on this course is unclear. Most historians once believed he decided only after a two-week Midwestern speaking tour convinced him in early October that the public wanted the Philippines. More plausibly, the taciturn Ohioan had determined to annex the archipelago long before and then waited for the people to catch up before making his decision public. As the war began, McKinley wrote in a personal memorandum, "While we are conducting war and until its conclusion we must keep all we get; when the war is over we must keep what we want." On June 24 Henry Cabot Lodge wrote Roosevelt that McKinley "wants to hold" the Philippines "but is a little timid about it." More likely he worried about the timidity of others.

McKinley the imperialist also was a politician. Both professions in a democracy demanded sensitivity to public opinion. First, his October tour convinced him not only that it was politically safe to annex the Philippines but a popularity bonanza. Second, he used the tour to coax the public into sharing his already formed views. His style of leadership dictated that he accomplish this by seeming to follow the people; he wanted them to think annexing the Philippines had been their idea. Thus, when the crowds roared their support of administration policies, it was in response to his own loaded questions: "Shall we deny to ourselves what the rest of the world so freely and so justly accords us?" George Boutwell, an observant anti-imperialist, saw what was happening: "the Speeches that the President is making . . . indicate [his] purposes to demand the Philippines as the price of peace with Spain." Lewis Gould believes McKinley purposely adopted a pose of indecision, "while simultaneously shaping events aimed at full American control after the peace treaty was signed." If Robert Hilderbrand is correct, he was being even more devious, refusing to announce his views for fear that public acceptance would freeze the territorial possibilities in half stride if it came too early. The public's acceptance of imperialism must first ripen further. "Mr. President, you didn't put my motion for a naval base," complained Secretary of State Day after a July cabinet meeting. "No, Judge," the president responded, "I was afraid it would be carried!"

Though McKinley did not favor annexation for a lack of alternatives, any chief executive would have found it hard to abandon the Philippines once troops had occupied Manila. Mr. Dooley told Hennessy, "We've got the Ph'lippeens, . . . we've got thim the way Casey got the bulldog—be th' teeth." Almost nobody favored returning the islands to Spain. A protectorate seemed unsuitable, since it would place heavy duties on the United States without supplying enough authority to carry them out. Only a few antiimperialists favored immediate independence for the Filipino "republic," which Aguinaldo proclaimed in June 1898. Most Americans believed freeing the islands would result in internal chaos followed by a German, British, or Japanese takeover. The potential diplomatic complications of U.S. withdrawal would itself be formidable. No country made a serious attempt to deny the Philippines to the United States, but at least four might have collided headlong if Washington turned them loose. British leaders urged Americans to bite the bullet and take the Philippines but made it clear they would want them otherwise. Japan applauded U.S. possession, partly to seek blessing for her activities in Korea, but especially to emphasize her opposition to any other power gaining control over the islands. Similarly, Russia saw nothing to protest in American policy but feared that Britain might somehow end up with a new edge. The driest tinder in the Philippines box was Germany. The commanders of the large German naval contingent observing the goings-on in Manila were openly discourteous to Dewey though under strict orders to cause no trouble. More than any other capital, Berlin was prepared to make a powerful grab for the Philippines if the Americans backed off.

These stumbling blocks might have blocked a president bent on getting rid of the Philippines, but McKinley was not. First, moral and ideological elements occupied him, as illustrated by the famous account of his decision on the Philippines. "I am not ashamed to tell you, gentlemen," he confessed to a delegation of fellow Methodists in a statement that should command more respect than it has usually received, "that I went down on my knees and prayed Almighty God for light and guidance more than one night." Late one of those nights, he continued, the reasons favoring annexation came to him, the ultimate one being, "That there was nothing left for us to do but to take them all, and to educate the Filipinos, and uplift and civilize and Christianize them and by God's grace do the very best we could by them, as our fellow men, for whom Christ also died." But McKinley had more prosaic motives, too. He wished to strengthen America's foothold in East Asia, and from the Philippines the United States could better defend its commercial interests in China and improve its political maneuverability in the entire region. In the words of an officer of the American Asiatic Association, an influential business lobby: "Had we no interests in China, the possession of the Philippines would be meaningless." The U.S. Naval Board looked on a base in the Philippines as an outpost of incalculable value in protecting American interests in China against European intrigues. McKinley's men had arrived at this position on their own, one summing up the argument in his description of the Philippines as America's "pickets of the Pacific, standing guard at the entrances to trade with the millions of China and Korea, French Indo-China, the Malay Peninsula, and the islands of Indonesia."

McKinley's clarity about what he wanted reflected the coming of the New Paradigm, which could be seen elsewhere as well. The once lax U.S. government tightened the sinews of administration and put soft sentiments behind it. The naval board just mentioned carried out effective intelligence and espionage activities throughout the war. From Newport the Naval War College, alert to the connections between issues, requested the seizure of Guam immediately after Dewey's victory at Manila, and Secretary of the Navy John D. Long sent the orders forthwith. The same Long, a redoubtably nonmilitaristic man, in June 1898 leaked Washington's intention to stage a raid on Spain's coast if a Spanish fleet were not recalled from a mission to relieve Dewey's hold on Manila. Long explained that he also wished "to awaken Europe to the fact that the republic of the western hemisphere did not hesitate to carry war, if necessary, across the Atlantic," surely an example of Great Power muscle-flexing. Similarly, McKinley spurned entreaties from his own generals to allow Spanish armies in Cuba to surrender on the most honorable terms possible: the president demanded a clear-cut capitulation to impress the nations of Europe. After the war, officials wrote legislation to create a permanent army of 100,000 men, looking ahead to more demands from a perilous world.

This project was not carried out, but it marked a new seriousness of purpose. So too did McKinley's close control of the war itself. "A serious strategist," David R. Trask has written, "who effectively related the use of force to the achievement of larger political goals," he directed military decisions from a specially outfitted White House War Room. The president's personal secretary, George Cortelyou, described him as "the strong man of the Cabinet, the dominating force" throughout the war. Though never an impressive leader in domestic affairs, McKinley firmly grasped the reins of military and diplomatic power, using a sophisticated communications system centered in White House offices. Fully exploiting both the telephone and telegraph, he exercised daily, even hour-to-hour, oversight of his commanders. He could exchange messages with General William R. Shafter in Cuba in twenty minutes. McKinley censored news of troop movements. The press, dependent on the White House for all important news, became vulnerable to manipulation. Thus, the White House released torrents of information about successes in the Philippines while obscuring news about foul-ups in Florida that delayed the invasion of Cuba. Later, the new secretary of state, John Hay, established regular news conferences as another means of controlling information and, thereby, public opinion. "Following the lead of the White House," writes Robert C. Hilderbrand, "the Department of State was becoming, at the end of the nineteenth century, an important source of information—and influence—for the press."

Precisely because McKinley's decisions seemed so far-reaching, they produced strenuous resistance from anti-imperialists, adherents to an earlier paradigm. The opponents of American imperialism included members of both political parties, leading political independents, businessmen, writers and intellectuals, and a few labor leaders and progressives. Among the more notable were Grover Cleveland, William Jennings Bryan, Thomas B. Reed, Benjamin Harrison, Carl Schurz, E. L. Godkin, Andrew Carnegie, Mark Twain, William Dean Howells, William James, Samuel Gompers, and Jane Addams. The most vocal and energetic were a group of elderly New England independents. Although the Spanish-American War had caused much head-shaking among them, the imperialist moves that followed, especially the annexation of the Philippines, galvanized their opposition.

Historians of the "economic" school have discounted the sincerity of the anti-imperialists. William A. Williams, for example, described them as "men who understood and advocated the very kind of informal empire created by the inherent imbalance of the marketplace relationship between the advanced industrial Metropolis and the poor, backward, agrarian societies." They opposed formal, map-altering colonialism because informal means of control would suffice for American socio-economic needs, cost less, and involve the nation in fewer messy encounters with "lesser breeds." This appraisal is one-sided at the very best. As this author in *Twelve Against Empire: The Anti-Imperialists, 1898–1900* (1968 and 1985) and others have demonstrated, few anti-imperialists paid much attention to economic issues. The core of their dismay was a belief that imperialism flatly contradicted American moral and political traditions. They feared that imperialist practices abroad would erode freedom at home. They deemed it immoral and unprincipled for the United States to deny freedom to the Philippines for the sake of its own ambitions. Seeing great dangers in Far Eastern diplomatic commitments and equal peril in trying to absorb "alien races" into the U.S. political system, anti-imperialists resisted both. Many were desolated by a sense that this imperial adventure marked the failure of the national mission, melancholy proof that America no longer stood above other nations in morality and wisdom. Although anti-imperialists failed in their short-term goals, their sharp attacks on the justifications for imperialism caused defensiveness in administration circles and chipped away at public support for colonialism.

Anti-imperialists found the horrors of the Filipino insurrection (or the Philippine-American War) particularly appalling. On December 21, 1898, McKinley proclaimed sovereignty over the Philippines, even though the Treaty of Paris was yet to be ratified. American policy in the islands, he declared, would strive for "benevolent assimilation." Many if not all Filipinos wanted independence instead, and fighting broke out in February 1899 after U.S. army commanders convinced Emilio Aguinaldo's followers of American ill-will. Three years were required to put down the last vestiges of rebellion. Nearly 130,000 U.S. troops served in this forgotten war, with a peak strength of 70,000; more than 4,000 were killed and 2,800 wounded in action, a remarkably high casualty figure. The Filipinos suffered more. Around 18,000 of their soldiers were killed and between 100,000 and 200,000 noncombatants died on the sidelines in torched villages, from famine in Spanish-style reconcentration camps, and from war-related diseases. Further souring the taste of America's imperial apple were shocking and all-too-true reports of widespread U.S. atrocities against both soldiers and civilians.

Ironically, reports of the uprising arrived in Washington just in time to help save the Paris peace treaty, which the Senate narrowly approved 57–27 on February 9, 1899. Two votes the other way and McKinley would have faced a major defeat (but not a fatal one, for he could resubmit the treaty to the more pliant Congress produced in the fall elections of 1898). Another factor in the treaty's passage was William Jennings Bryan's surprising support, justified to eliminate Spain from the picture, free the United States to grant independence to the Philippines, and release Bryan to focus on domestic issues in the 1900 election campaign. Paolo E. Coletta contends that Bryan's strategy influenced few if any senators to favor ratification. Yet at least two of the nineteen Democrats and silverite allies who supported the treaty would almost certainly have abandoned (and thus defeated) it had Bryan come out foursquare against the pact as a party issue. On the Republican side, only two New Englanders of anti-imperialist sympathies voted against the treaty. Many others harbored misgivings but were held in line by effective lobbying and patronage bribes. The fragility of support for administration policy became apparent eight days after ratification when only twenty-nine votes could be mustered against a resolution calling for an end to American control over the Philippines as soon as they established "a stable and independent government. . . ." Since the resolution also attracted only twenty-nine supporters, Vice-President Garret Hobart was able to kill it with his tie-breaking vote.

Some critics, including anti-imperialists, charged McKinley with allowing the United States to be lured into the Far East to serve British rather than U.S. interests. This criticism underestimated the government's capacity to adopt policies for its own good reasons, one of which, carried out in the teeth of vocal opposition, was to forge closer ties with Great Britain. Her goodwill during the war, her rebuff of a German proposal that the United States relinquish its position in either Hawaii or Samoa, and her applause for the decision to annex the Philippines all seemed to justify the hands-across-the-sea enthusiasm that swept up many Americans. Leaders of both governments took pains to cultivate the mood. Britain's colonial secretary Joseph Chamberlain wrote John Hay in 1898: "I should rejoice in an occasion in which we could fight side by side. The good effect of it would last for generations." And Hay, by then secretary of state, remarked a year later: "As long as I stay here, no action shall be taken contrary to my conviction that the indispensable feature of our foreign policy should be a friendly understanding with England."

Concrete results of this rapprochement were few but important. Congress quashed legislation hostile to British shipping interests. British diplomats and naval officers cooperated with the Americans in the Philippine-American war. And despite strong pro-Boer sentiment among the American people, the U.S. government conducted a neutrality policy during the Boer War that tilted sharply toward Britain. Thomas J. Noer, in *Briton, Boer, and Yankee: The United States and South Africa, 1870–1914* (1978), sees Washington acting out the elements of the New Paradigm in South Africa: continuous U.S. support for the British from the mid-eighties onward, awareness of the connections between war in South Africa and issues elsewhere in the world, readiness to both shape and ignore domestic public opinion for policy goals, and strong centralized control in the state department. In view of American friendship, the British admiralty in 1901 decided that all naval building plans should henceforth hypothesize a friendly U.S. fleet. The most significant product of rapprochement was the long-awaited settlement of the canal question. The Hay-Pauncefote Treaty of 1901 canceled the vexatious Clayton-Bulwer Treaty of 1850 and endowed the United States with the right to build, fortify, and control a canal of its own. In an orgy of amendments the Senate had so mutilated a 1900 version of the treaty that the British rejected it as humiliating, yet the agreement they accepted in 1901 was virtually the one insisted on by the Senate. In this instance, Hay and McKinley showed a less acute awareness of what the national interest required than their critics (including Theodore Roosevelt), who demanded elimination of provisions to neutralize the canal in war and to allow other powers to join in guaranteeing the canal's neutrality.

The senators and T.R. got their way, not only because Britain knew the Senate might unilaterally abrogate the Clayton-Bulwer Treaty if they didn't, but also because the agony of the Boer War and other events had left her with few friends in Europe. Many observers believed the Anglo-American rapprochement stemmed exclusively from mutual or parallel interests in Asia and the Caribbean. But in retrospect its most important source was the decline of British supremacy in Europe and America's rise in the Western Hemisphere. Britain, not the United States, gave in during the Venezuela crisis. Britain conceded American supremacy in Hawaii and the Caribbean, surrendered its isthmian canal rights, and in 1903 yielded, yet again, on the Alaska-Canadian boundary dispute. Alert to this pattern, John Hay wrote in 1900: "All I have ever done with England is to have wrung great concessions out of her with no compensation." Which is precisely how his countrymen thought it should be. Partly because suspicions persisted among anti-imperialists, German and Irish immigrants, isolationists, and other unreconstructed Anglophobes, the new transatlantic friendship was tenuous at best, marked, Charles S.

Campbell, Jr., writes, by a "forced, hothouse quality" that could not outlive "wartime emotionalism. . . ." Many Anglo-American disagreements still lay in the future.

THE OPEN DOOR POLICY

For many years historians interpreted the Open Door notes of 1899–1900—the last major episode in this era of U.S. diplomacy—as a British invention, a fruit of rapprochement. In reality, the "Open Door Policy" emerged from traditional views on the Far East when Washington decided it must preserve U.S. interests amid the carving up of China. Besides trade and investments, America's new standing as a world power was at stake: how would the United States look if it stood idly by while China was cut to pieces? Finally, McKinley and Hay were powerfully infected by Importance-of-Asia Syndrome. In 1897, Captain Mahan remarked that "in Asia, not in Europe, is now the greatest danger to our proximate interests." This view became more pronounced in 1898, even though nothing terrible had yet happened to the "proximate interests" in question. The United States was now a great power, and all those powers possessed Far Eastern policies. Officials greatly exaggerated the importance East Asia then had to the United States; "objectively," Europe would long have more impact on American political, economic, and cultural life. Yet those in power had little doubt that American interests in Asia were vital. It was to Asia, not to Europe, that they sent warships and occupation troops; it was in Asia where they grimly held on to colonial territory in the face of war and division at home; and in Asia that the United States would join other outsiders in suppressing the Boxer Rebellion.

As to concrete interests, Washington officials worried far less about various capital-investment projects (few in number and often thought to be more trouble than they were worth) than the growing market in China for U.S.

Concln

exports—especially cotton textiles, illuminating oil, flour, lumber, and iron and steel products. The amounts of money involved were unimpressive compared either to British exports to China or American sales to other countries. American exports to China, however, had doubled in value from 1896 to 1899 and ranked second to Britain's. By 1900 this market seemed crucial to the cotton textiles industry, following a decade in which exports to China had risen from a little more than $7 million to nearly $24 million, almost 50 percent of the industry's foreign sales. Moreover, Americans who calculated the importance of U.S. interests in China thought less of current trade levels than they dreamed of a grandiose future ("a shirt on every Chinaman's back").

The imperialist scavengers fell on the Chinese carcass in the autumn of 1897. Within six months, beginning with Germany's seizure of Kiaochow in November, five nations extorted leaseholds and spheres of influence from the beleaguered Chinese: Germany and Russia in Manchuria, North China, and the Shantung Peninsula; Great Britain in Shantung, Kowloon (opposite Hong Kong), and the Yangtze Valley; Japan in Fukien province across the straits from her new possession of Formosa; and France near her holdings in Indochina. What American officials would do—nervous about the economy, newly inclined to espy vital U.S. interests in Asia and translate views into action—was unclear at first. But the issues were clear enough, especially in northern China and Manchuria where two-thirds of American exports to China were sold and where Germany and Russia now seemed firmly ensconced. What should they do, Washington officials asked one another, if Chinese ports were closed to American goods, or discriminatory harbor duties were placed on the vessels carrying them? What if unequal tariffs were imposed on U.S. products? What if higher freight rates were charged for carrying American goods to the interior than for those of the country controlling the interior?

At first, Washington seemed sanguine, Secretary of

State John Sherman even suggesting that a partition of China might boost American profits. Sherman, however, never spoke for the core of the McKinley administration. Other officials noted the concern expressed by big-city chambers of commerce, newspapers, and especially the group of businessmen organized as the Committee on American Interests in China. Though this concern may have had some effect, McKinley's administration had been busy on its own, trying to expand the areas where American businessmen could live in China, soliciting commercial information from missionaries, encouraging China to take part in trade expositions, and vainly urging Peking to eliminate barriers in trade among provinces within China. The U.S. government did not then want its own sphere of influence. Adopting this great-power tactic would start the anti-imperialist hornets buzzing again and create new problems for men whose hands were already full with novel tasks. Besides, Russia and Germany had just fenced off the areas where American businessmen had enjoyed their greatest success; thus, surveying for a new homestead on untried soil looked less than promising. Besides, as Thomas J. McCormick has written, "a small slice of the pie (which is all partitioning could offer) held little attraction for men who wanted (and thought they could get) the major share of the [entire Chinese] market."

In March 1898 Great Britain suggested united action to preserve the open door, but Washington politely rejected the overture. The Cuban affair, about to culminate in war, required all its attention; in any case, the United States still preferred to act alone rather than in league with others. By the summer of 1899, however, strong U.S. action had come to seem feasible and desirable. The war with Spain was over and the peace treaty ratified. Ownership of the Philippines bolstered confidence in the capacity for bold action and, along with a fresh spate of magazine and newspaper articles on Chinese affairs, stimulated public interest in China. Pressure from businessmen mounted. Finally, the China kaleidoscope ceased revolving just as Britain, Japan, and Germany looked ready and even eager for some kind of open-door understanding. This left Russia, bristling menacingly in Manchuria.

Action

John Hay's problem was finding a way to get Russia in step without risking a rebuff damaging to U.S. prestige and the open door principle. In August 1899, St. Petersburg hinted at an endorsement of equal commercial opportunities in the Russian zone. Hay pounced on this opening, though the Russian ukase said nothing about railroad rates, and on September 6 sent off the first Open Door notes, drafted by William W. Rockhill, his Far Eastern adviser. The first group went to Germany, Russia, and Great Britain, others later to Japan, France, and Italy. Hay asked each power with a sphere of influence or leasehold to subscribe to four key points: (1) keep all "treaty" ports open; (2) maintain China's own tariff rates indiscriminately on all foreign goods, including those of the "local" imperial power; (3) impose no discriminatory harbor dues on ships of other nationalities; and (4) maintain nondiscriminatory railroad charges in the sphere's (or leasehold's) interior.

points

A phrase calling on China to collect its own customs revenue suggested to some historians that Hay was obliquely trying to undermine the whole spheres-of-influence system. This is unlikely considering that he never consulted with China until after Peking made pointed inquiries. Far from challenging the system of spheres of influence, he endeavored to protect American interests within it. The language of the first of the Open Door notes was precise: they applied only to the areas controlled by foreign powers, not to China at large. Nor did they say anything about railroads, mines, or other capital-investment issues. Even though Hay termed his demands modestly, if they won acceptance he could claim a low-cost triumph for American diplomacy and the fortunes of McKinley and the Republican Party. A singular flaw in the policy, however, made it vulnerable to failure: no one, including Hay, was prepared to use force, or even the threat of force, to keep the open door. The New Paradigm of 1899 did not encompass that level of risk-taking in Asia.

All would depend on the reaction to the notes. As this story was once told, none of the powers accepted Hay's terms, but he publicly announced that they had done so—a move described by admirers as an inspired diplomatic stroke that caught the great powers off balance and forced them into line, but by critics as ineffectual and misleading to the American people. By contrast, more recent accounts such as Thomas J. McCormick's *China Market: America's Quest for Informal Empire, 1893–1901* (1967) establish that Hay managed the entire affair with impressive subtlety if mixed results. Working on the easiest marks first and reserving the Russians for last, he supervised separate talks with each power, hoping to avoid the one outright "No" that would cancel the assents of others. His tactics aimed at creating a momentum of unanimous agreement ("If everyone else goes along, I will, too."). Britain accepted his terms in general but not specifically for Hong Kong or Kowloon; she also insisted that the other powers agree, too. Japan, Italy, and France all accepted quickly but with conditions. Germany added a qualified assent only after much grumbling. The Russians now found themselves in a corner. Their position in Manchuria was too insecure to allow a policy of flat rejection; they could not afford arousing everyone's suspicions by undoing all the others' (conditional) acceptances. They stalled, they argued tenaciously, but they finally "accepted" early in 1900.

The Russian response was elaborately hedged and did not even allude to the question of railroad rates. What to do? Hay first tried pressing the Russians, but they relented only to the point of permitting him to describe their reply as "favorable." Hay leaped into the dark. On March 20, despite the absence of a single unconditionally positive reply, the secretary of state announced that Washington had received "favorable" responses from all parties. Though a bluff of sorts, this was not the reckless trick of which he has been accused. Nor, contrary to once-popular views, had he deluded himself into thinking he had "saved" China. Hay understood, moreover, that limited U.S. interests and cautious public sentiments meant the United States would have to stand aside if Russia or Japan chose to remold the Asian balance of power by seizing control in China.

The difficulty in making a low-cost policy profitable became clear in 1900 during the Boxer Rebellion, which threatened to trigger a new round of partitions. Spearheaded by youths but connived at by Chinese officials and the dowager empress herself, the rebellion resulted in widespread looting and murders of foreigners, especially Christian missionaries. The Boxers killed several of the "barbarians" in Peking's foreign quarter, including the German minister, before laying siege to it. U.S. Minister Edwin Conger begged Washington to cooperate with the other powers in a rescue expedition, but the administration—dodging the slings and arrows of anti-imperialists at home and tracking down Aguinaldo's rebels in the Philippines—hesitated. McKinley was loath to abandon an independent stance in Chinese affairs. Nor did he wish to do anything to encourage further partitions or occupations of China. But he finally decided that even greater danger to both U.S. prestige and commerce lay in allowing others to dominate the expedition. Ignoring Congress, McKinley ordered about 5,000 troops from the Philippines to join a combined force of 19,000, which finally broke the siege in mid-August 1900. Diplomat Henry White wrote, "I am very glad to see that we are . . . acting generally as a great power with our vast commercial interest should."

(Although, ironically, the war in the Philippines made it difficult to spare the manpower for the Boxer expedition, being able to send troops at all illustrated precisely what the advocates of Philippines annexation had in mind. Hay warmed to the subject in a letter to the president in July of 1900: "On the possession of the Philippines rests that admirable diplomacy which warned all nations that American trade was not to be shut out of China. It is to Manila that we owe the abilities to send our troops and ships in defense of our ministers, our missionaries, our consuls, and our merchants in China, instead of being compelled to leave our citizens to the casual protection of other powers, as would have been unavoidable had we flung the Philippines away. . . . It is to Manila, again, to our fleet in the bay and our army on the land, that we shall owe our power, when these scenes of blood in China are closed, to exact reparation, to enforce stern justice, and to insist in the final settlement, upon an open door to all that vast market of our fast growing commerce. Events coming with terrible rapidity, have made swift witnesses to the wisdom of our action in the East.'')

On July 3, 1900, Hay sent out his second Open Door note, this time a circular requiring no response. On its face, this note seemed a decided expansion of the U.S. commitment in China, both in referring to the open door principle as applying to ''all parts of the Chinese Empire'' and in declaring it American policy to ''preserve Chinese territorial and administrative entity. . . .'' Hay was no fool, however, and his purposes were much more limited than his words indicated. He was painfully aware how unwilling his countrymen were to back up his diplomatic language. This time he probably wished only to encourage moderate conduct among the Boxer expedition allies by setting a proper example with a public avowal that Washington would not exploit the crisis by trying to weaken the Chinese state or obstruct the open door. The note rested on the hope that none of the other powers would risk disrupting the balance of power in Asia (or Europe) by a determined thrust for exclusive control in China. Michael H. Hunt has pointed to the note's caution: it ''posed no challenge to the unequal treaties . . . or the existing foreign concessions and spheres of influence. . . .'' Suggesting a yet more modest purpose was the memorandum Assistant Secretary of State John Bassett Moore sent Hay just two days before the latter issued his circular, in which Moore declared America's "immediate interest" in Asia to be that of watching out for the security of the *Philippines*. Finally, the second Open Door note probably had an internal purpose as well—to squelch the navy's intrigues for a Chinese base of its own. Oddly, in November 1900, four months after he sent the circular, Hay made a bid to get Samsa Bay (opposite Formosa) for the United States, quickly retracting the request, however, in the face of Japanese objections. This abortive episode once more exposes the Open Door policy as one that neither challenged foreign spheres of influence in China nor precluded Washington's acquiring one. It also suggests that however many strides U.S. diplomacy had made in system and seriousness, the China tangle could still sow confusion in American policymaking.

The protocol negotiations that followed the suppression of the rebellion exposed the weakness of the American position. Almost alone, the United States advocated moderate punishment for the Chinese. The final protocol of September 1901, however, reflected the harsh mood of the other powers, calling for the punishment and in some cases execution of various Chinese parties, the erection of monuments where foreigners had been murdered and other outrages taken place, a guarantee of an unfettered line of communications from Peking to the sea for foreigners, and reparations of a third of a billion dollars. Nothing was said about enforcing the open door. In Henry Cabot Lodge's opinion the Chinese issue was "the gravest and most difficult question which this or any other generation has confronted," but when Japan asked how much the United States might do for the open door, Hay replied that his government was not contemplating the use of force, either unilaterally or in league with others.

This unwillingness to back the open door with force explains why many historians have attacked the policy, but others have criticized it because it committed the United States to peripheral and indefensible goals, and because it rested on the flimsy belief that other powers shared America's desire for an open China. Critics have also repeatedly argued that the caution of the great powers—making certain that an Asian conflict would not spark what could have been a world war—not Hay's policy, did most to stay the further dismemberment of China.

Some of these criticisms are unfair in exaggerating what McKinley and Hay hoped to achieve. In their defense, Thomas J. McCormick makes the point that attempting to support the open door with a mix of rhetoric, timely overtures, and minimal commitment of force was not really so quixotic when a "de facto balance of power" existed in China, with Russia and France on one side, and Britain and Japan on the other. Under these circumstances, "there was a good chance the powers would acquiesce" if the United States, acting as a "third force," "dramatically insisted that the status quo . . . be universally accepted. . . ." The path of retreat always remained open if the going got rough, as it had by 1900, when Hay spoke of "hold[ing] on like grim death to the Open Door." Though sorry not to accomplish more, he knew better than to try to defend an untenable position; when other powers showed more willingness to take risks, he pulled back, muzzling chatter about upholding China's "integrity" as he did so. It was well that Hay knew when to retreat because, in clumsier hands, the Open Door policy could be disastrous, based as it was on a set of fantasies; in this the critics are certainly right. Marilyn B. Young has written that "the notion of a special friendship between China and America, of the riches of the China market, of America's role as balancer of powers in Asia, were all accepted as descriptions of the situation and not, as they were in fact, the possibilities merely. The American public was given to believe that its most vital national interests were involved in China, yet the commercial and financial interests which might have given substance to this claim were absent." The Open Door had become a major United States "policy" because of the world view produced by the

New Paradigm. Appearing important in the eyes of American leaders did not require that China be "objectively" important. "Americans looked to China for justification of their new self-image," writes Robert McClellan; "therefore it mattered little if the policy of the United States in China was based on actual conditions. What did matter was that any policy had to be formulated in accord with the concept of America's new role in world affairs."

During McKinley's successful reelection campaign in 1900, Republicans scurried to avow their innocence of the un-American crime of "imperialism." The GOP platform declared that "no thought of national aggrandizement has tarnished the high purpose" of the United States. Senator Lodge, though rejecting the accusation of "imperialism," did admit to favoring "expansion," which he took to be a positive good. McKinley's running mate Theodore Roosevelt asserted that "nothing even remotely resembling 'imperialism' or 'militarism' " had been involved in recent events, which he thought of as a new phase "of that policy of expansion which has been part of the history of America from the day when she became a nation." These men may have been deceiving themselves, but with considerable sincerity, just as they meant it when disclaiming any plans for further territorial aggrandizement. The outstanding hallmark of the McKinley administration was not a headlong rush toward colonialism but the inauguration of America's new career as a world power, part of the advent of a new paradigm of diplomacy. An assassin erased any further part for McKinley in this transformation, but Roosevelt carried on—"the first president," H. Wayne Morgan writes, "to have no rest from complicated foreign issues, just as his generation of Americans was the first to pursue more than 'crisis diplomacy.' Foreign affairs were here to stay."

Harbingers

In 1900 the United States stood face to face with many issues that would dominate the American diplomatic agenda in the twentieth century. No one yet lost sleep over Soviet communism or the impact of air power and atomic weapons on national security; the United States had not yet been ensnared in the deadly web of European diplomacy that would soon result in "the Great War." Yet many enduring patterns were already in place. American and Russian interests collided in Manchuria, challenging the myth of a "natural" friendship between the two nations. The foundation of amicable relations with Germany had crumbled away owing to friction over Samoa, the Philippines, and China. United States ties with Britain, on the other hand, had become predictably friendly, despite an occasional misunderstanding. Relations with China wavered back and forth for years, from lukewarm to cordial, but a steady trend of

154

greater antagonism with Japan was already visible. Generally, the evolution of U.S. policy toward the Far East in the years after 1898 can be viewed as puzzle-solving activity within the New Paradigm—as diplomatic experiments conducted to find the best means for achieving agreed-upon goals. Was it taken for granted that the United States must protect vital commercial and political interests in Asia as a way to protect American security? Then the Philippines-American War suggested that colonialism was not the best path to the objective. What, then, about the Open Door notes? Not too bad, but still not reliably effective. Perhaps the United States could accomplish its ends, Theodore Roosevelt decided, by abandoning the essence of the Open Door and finding space for American interests between Russia and Japan as they struggled for Asian supremacy. American diplomatists would long continue their experiments in the diplomatic laboratories; rarely, however, would they emerge to rethink the need for a significant U.S. presence in East Asia.

Three developments around the turn of the century would hamstring America's freedom of action in Asian policymaking. The first was acquiring the Philippines, which nailed down the United States to an unprecedented military commitment in the Far East. The second was the Open Door policy, which, as it unfolded under some of Hay's successors, increasingly cast the United States as the defender of China. The third was the growing belief that events in Asia had a vital bearing on United States interests—that Americans would gain economic sustenance and political influence in Asia in exchange for guiding China into the new world of democracy, Christianity, and commerce.

All three pointed toward conflict with Japan.

Relations between the United States and Latin America also proceeded logically from the base formed in the 1890s. Americans had long had a special interest in this region but without benefit of a clear "policy." Periodically but without pattern the United States would make a grab at nearby territory or meddle in the affairs of a troubled Latin republic. American policy toward the hemisphere congealed in the nineties, auguring future U.S. dominance in the area, particularly the Caribbean. The new sense of direction derived mainly from the need to protect the isthmian canal, which was finally constructed after the Panamanian revolution of 1903. In 1904, Roosevelt's Corollary to the Monroe Doctrine formalized the new policy, and a series of interventions during the next twenty years proved Washington's seriousness in enforcing it. By the end of the Wilson administration, the United States had become not only the uncontested arbiter of Caribbean questions, but the region's semicolonial master as well.

This mastery was not brought about by seizing new colonies, for the surge of American colonialism ended in 1900. The anti-imperialist movement had put outright colonialists on the defensive; businessmen quickly lost their interest in formal empire; and, as Goran Rystad notes, "the protracted and bloody war in the Philippines led to many formerly convinced expansionists having second thoughts." In any case, the leaders of the McKinley administration had never defined colonialism as an essential object of U.S. policy. Instead they had worked to expand American political and economic interests generally. To achieve this goal they gave unprecedented attention to the systematic formulation and execution of U.S. foreign policy. In doing so, they inaugurated a new era in American diplomatic history.

It goes beyond the scope of this book to describe how the 1890s policy paradigm was later succeeded by other, similarly abrupt, changes in American diplomatic patterns, though Michael Roskin suggests that such breaks occurred after World War I and the Versailles Treaty, again after Munich and Pearl Harbor, and most recently in the late 1960s when the Vietnam War provoked a profound reaction against the global pretensions and fears that were the hallmark of American foreign policy in the years from Franklin Roosevelt to Lyndon Johnson.

For better or worse, some of the changes of the 1890s remain a part of American foreign policy to our own day. Since 1900 the United States government has never conducted diplomacy in the amateurish manner that was par for the course in the 1870s and 1880s (though professional competence should not be equated with wisdom). No administration since 1900—including those of Harding, Coolidge, and Hoover—has tried returning to the isolationist dicta of a Rutherford Hayes. And no president since McKinley has ignored the Far East with the aplomb of a Chester Arthur, or even a Grover Cleveland. The Harrisons, Blaines, Olneys, McKinleys, and Hays could not anticipate what would come in the next eighty-five years, but they knew they had led the United States into a new and dangerous world of power politics. The prospect seemed to excite more than to disturb them.

Bibliographical Essay

In the interests of saving space, I have abbreviated the names of some scholarly journals, as follows:

AHR (American Historical Review)
DH (Diplomatic History)
HAHR (Hispanic American Historical Review)
JAH (Journal of American History)
MVHR (Mississippi Valley Historical Review)
PHR (Pacific Historical Review)

My interpretation of this era relies heavily on the analyses and monographs of others. One of the most important is Walter LaFeber's *The New Empire: An Interpretation of American Expansion, 1860–1898* (Ithaca, 1963), sometimes one-dimensional in its psychology and excessively dependent on an economic model of explanation, but invaluable nonetheless, the first scholarly work to link the dramatic events of 1898 to the generation preceding. This work, along with H. Wayne Morgan's *From Hayes to McKinley: National Party Politics, 1877–1896* (Syracuse, 1969) and Milton Plesur's *America's Outward Thurst: Approaches to Foreign Affairs, 1865–1890* (DeKalb, Ill., 1971) go far to remove the label of mediocrity from this transforming era of American history. Plesur's work, though otherwise unexciting, devotes unusual attention to such routine diplomatic subjects as the protection of U.S. citizens abroad, the quotidian behavior of aspiring exporters, and such unofficial phases of foreign relations as tourism. Despite its title, the volume focuses almost exclusively on the 1880s. Another sober work, showing how the impulse toward increased reliance on state power was restrained by tradition and localism, is Morton Keller, *Affairs of State: Public Life in Late Nineteenth Century America* (Cambridge, Mass., 1977).

Several other works strongly influenced me as I shaped my own analysis of this period. Richard Hofstadter's subtle essay, "Cuba, the Philippines, and Manifest Destiny," in *The Paranoid Style in American Politics and Other Essays* (New York, 1965; the essay was originally published in 1952), first drew my attention to the "crisis" of the 1890s. Two works demonstrated the inseparability of economic, political, and ideological impulses: David Healy, *US Expansionism: The Imperialist Urge in the 1890s* (Madison, 1970), and James A. Field, Jr., *America and the Mediterranean World, 1776–1882* (Princeton, 1969). Eclectic in viewpoint, Healy's examination of the expedient use of "markets" rhetoric by men whose primary interests were in national power casts doubt on the significance of rhetorical evidence cited by LaFeber and others. Field's volume elegantly analyzes the ideological foundations underlying America's emphasis on exports and shipping (as well as revealing the weakness of the "center" in controlling policy in the sixties and seventies).

As readers of this book know, Thomas S. Kuhn's *The Structure of Scientific Revolutions* (2d ed., Chicago, 1970) provided me with the interpretive model for understanding the diplomatic "revolution" of the 1890s. More on how Kuhn arrived at his model, in addition to his second thoughts, are available in *The Essential Tension: Selected Studies in Scientific Tradition and Change* (Chicago, 1977). The first work in which I saw the paradigm analysis applied persuasively to diplomatic history was Michael Roskin's "Turning Inward: The Effects of the Vietnam War on U.S. Foreign Policy" (Ph.D. dissertation, The American University, 1972). Almost equally influential in forming my views was Robert H. Wiebe's *The Search for Order, 1877–1920* (New York, 1967), which, aside from its significant interpretation of American history generally, incorporates a trenchant analysis of the piecemeal character of U.S. diplomacy before the age of "policy." An enormously suggestive work, it leaves unclear why the shift from "incidents" to "policy" occurred and dates the arrival of the change later than I have in this volume.

Analyses not derived from Kuhn but suggesting similar perceptions include a fascinating work by Alan K. Henrikson, "America's Changing Place in the World: From 'Periphery' to 'Centre'?" in Jean Gottmann, ed., *Centre and Periphery: Spatial Variation in Politics* (Beverly Hills, 1980); Ernest R. May, "The Nature of Foreign Policy: The Calculated vs. the Axiomatic," *Daedalus* 91 (Fall 1962); and— emphasizing why it is hard for policymakers to look ahead—Lincoln P. Bloomfield, "Planning Foreign Policy: Can It Be Done?" *Political Science Quarterly* 93 (Fall 1978). Stephen Skowronek's excellent book, *Building a New American State: The Expansion of National Administrative*

Capacities, 1877–1920 (Cambridge, U.K., 1982), though not concerned with diplomacy, is the source of Franz Neumann's statement.

Several other syntheses of this era deserve mention. Valuable for its detailed coverage but somewhat predictable is Charles S. Campbell, Jr.'s *The Transformation of American Foreign Relations, 1865–1900* (New York, 1976). Discussing a variety of subjects from the origins of the modern navy and the Venezuela crisis to the causes of war in 1898 is J. A. S. Grenville and G. B. Young, *Politics, Strategy and American Diplomacy: Studies in Foreign Policy, 1873–1917* (New Haven, 1966), which puts little stock in economic interpretations and probably too much in political explanations. A provocative, wide-ranging work on American cultural imperialism is Emily S. Rosenberg, *Spreading the American Dream: American Economic and Cultural Expansion, 1890–1945* (New York, 1982). A tame but sometimes useful synthesis is John M. Dobson, *America's Ascent: The United States Becomes a Great Power, 1880–1914* (DeKalb, Ill., 1978).

A guide to tensions among early American diplomatic traditions is Felix Gilbert, *To the Farewell Address: Ideas of Early American Foreign Policy* (Princteon, 1961). All those interested in American imperialism should eventually make their way through Albert K. Weinberg's mordant and erudite *Manifest Destiny: A Study of Nationalist Expansionism in American History* (Baltimore, 1935). For a stimulating discussion of Americans' inability to define and face up to "imperialism," see Robin W. Winks, "The Americans' Struggle with 'Imperialism': How Words Frighten," in Rob Kroes, ed., *The American Identity: Fusion and Fragmentation* (Amsterdam, 1980).

To gain a thorough grounding in the "markets" thesis, of which LaFeber's book is the most persuasive version, one should read William A. Williams's *The Tragedy of American Diplomacy* (2d ed., New York, 1972); *The Contours of American History* (Cleveland, 1961); and *The Roots of the*

Modern American Empire: A Study of the Growth and Shaping of Social Consciousness in a Marketplace Society (New York, 1969). These books are serious efforts to discover the roots of what their author sees as long-lived, tragic compulsions in American diplomacy. The main importance of the last work lies in the massively researched if tedious attempt to fold agriculture into the economic interpretation of American foreign policy. All of Williams's works contain passages of great power and insight; however, as critics have noted, his arguments are tendentious, his use of evidence questionable, and his disregard for conflicting scholarship cavalier. Among the critics, read Robert James Maddox's *The New Left and the Origins of the Cold War* (Princeton, 1973); and Richard A. Melanson, "The Social and Political Thought of William Appleman Williams," *Western Political Quarterly* 31 (September 1978). Critiques that focus more specifically on the issues at hand, and that are sometimes directed to historians other than Williams, include Paul S. Holbo, "Economics, Emotion, and Expansion: An Emerging Foreign Policy," in H. Wayne Morgan, ed., *The Gilded Age* (rev. ed., Syracuse, 1970); and David M. Pletcher, "1861–1898: Economic Growth and Diplomatic Adjustment," in William H. Becker and Samuel F. Wells, Jr., eds., *Economics and World Power: An Assessment of American Diplomacy Since 1789* (New York, 1984). Criticism and commentary on this issue continue in several works of William H. Becker, including *The Dynamics of Business-Government Relations: Industry & Exports, 1893–1921* (Chicago, 1982), which demonstrates the persistent businessmen's distrust of the federal government and attractiveness of domestic as well as foreign markets; "Foreign Markets for Iron and Steel, 1893–1913: A New Perspective on the Williams School of Diplomatic History," *PHR* 44 (May 1975), which argues that "the major thrust of activity to solve depression-related problems was domestic"; and "American Manufacturers and Foreign Markets, 1870–1900: Business Historians and the 'New Economic Determinists,' " *Business History Review*

47 (Winter 1973). Contradicting the view that foreign trade expansion was seen as the cure for the 1893 panic is Gerald T. White, *The United States and the Problem of Recovery after 1893* (University, Ala., 1982). Other related works are David E. Novack and Matthew Simon, "Commercial Responses to the American Export Invasion, 1871–1914: An Essay in Attitudinal History," *Explorations in Entrepreneurial History* 3, 2d ser. (Winter 1966); Stanley Lebergott, "The Returns to U.S. Imperialism, 1890–1929," *Journal of Economic History* 40 (June 1980); and Robert Zevin, "An Interpretation of American Imperialism," *Journal of Economic History* 32 (March 1972).

Studies abound of U.S. relations with particular countries and regions, though no decent synthesis exists of U.S.-European relations. American relations with Great Britain have drawn the most attention. Students should examine Kenneth Bourne, *Britain and the Balance of Power in North America, 1815–1908* (Berkeley, 1967); the invaluable if wordy H. C. Allen, *Great Britain and the United States* (New York, 1955); and Bradford Perkins's helpful survey, *The Great Rapprochement: England and the United States, 1895–1914* (New York, 1968). Four excellent books focusing on the Spanish-American War era are Lionel M. Gelber, *The Rise of Anglo-American Friendship: A Study in World Politics, 1898–1906* (London, 1938), partially outmoded but on firm ground in delineating the limits of the rapprochement; R. G. Neale, *Great Britain and United States Expansion: 1898–1900* (East Lansing, 1966); Charles S. Campbell, Jr., *Anglo-American Understanding, 1898–1903* (Baltimore, 1957); and Alexander E. Campbell, *Great Britain and the United States, 1895–1903* (London, 1960). Running against the tide of historiographical tradition, Edward P. Crapol's *America for Americans: Economic Nationalism and Anglophobia in the Late Nineteenth Century* (Westport, 1973) stresses conflict over rapprochement.

Other studies of U.S. relations with European nations include Henry Blumenthal's *A Reappraisal of Franco-*

American Relations, 1830–1871 (Chapel Hill, 1959) and *France and the United States: Their Diplomatic Relations, 1789–1914* (Chapel Hill, 1970); Manfred Jonas, *The United States and Germany: A Diplomatic History* (Ithaca, 1984); and James W. Cortada, *Two Nations Over Time: Spain and the United States, 1776–1977* (Westport, 1978), which is most valuable on the twentieth century.

Robert C. Brown's *Canada's National Policy, 1883–1900: A Study in Canadian-American Relations* (Princeton, 1964) is excellent. A number of accounts of U.S. relations with Latin America in general deserve attention. By far the most valuable for this study was Joseph Smith, *Illusions of Conflict: Anglo-American Diplomacy Toward Latin America, 1865–1896* (Pittsburgh, 1979), which relates the growing U.S. assertiveness and eventual supremacy in Latin America, achieved at the expense of a Britain that backed down gracefully. An able survey is Lester D. Langley, *Struggle for the American Mediterranean: United States-European Rivalry in the Gulf-Caribbean, 1776–1904* (Athens, Ga., 1976). Another informative work is Arthur P. Whitaker, *The United States and the Southern Cone: Argentina, Chile, and Uruguay* (Cambridge, Mass., 1976). For the history of the canal issue, see Gerstle Mack, *The Land Divided: A History of the Panama Canal and Other Isthmian Canal Projects* (New York, 1944); Mary W. Williams, *Anglo-American Isthmian Diplomacy, 1815–1915* (Washington, D.C., 1916); and David McCullough, *The Path Between the Seas: The Creation of the Panama Canal, 1870–1914* (New York, 1977). For a sectional perspective on the hemisphere, see Tennant S. McWilliams, "The Lure of Empire: Southern Interest in the Caribbean, 1877–1900," *Mississippi Quarterly* 29 (Winter 1975–76).

Among studies of U.S. relations with particular countries, the most useful to me were Karl M. Schmitt, *Mexico and the United States, 1821–1973: Conflict and Coexistence* (New York, 1974); G. M. Joseph, *Revolution from Without: Yucatán, Mexico, and the United States, 1880–1924* (Cambridge, U.K., 1982); Louis A. Pérez, Jr., *Cuba Between Empires, 1878-1902* (Pittsburgh, 1983), an important work putting Washington's hostility to Cuban revolutions in the foreground; Lester D. Langley, *The Cuban Policy of the United States: A Brief History* (New York, 1968); Philip S. Foner, *A History of Cuba and Its Relations with the United States*, 2 vols. (New York, 1963), an exaggerated version of the thesis argued more persuasively by Pérez; and Ludwell L. Montague, *Haiti and the United States, 1714-1938* (Durham, 1940).

Two old standbys covering U.S. relations with Asia are Tyler Dennett, *Americans in Eastern Asia* (New York, 1922); and A. Whitney Griswold, *The Far Eastern Policy of the United States* (New York, 1938). Though ostensibly concerned only with China, Michael H. Hunt's *The Making of a Special Relationship: The United States and China to 1914* (New York, 1983) is far superior. Researched in both English and Chinese sources, this fine book reminds us of the Chinese role in influencing the relationship of the two nations. Also important are Marilyn B. Young, *Rhetoric of Empire: American China Policy, 1895-1901* (Cambridge, Mass., 1968), and her "American Expansion 1870-1900: The Far East," in Barton J. Bernstein, ed., *Towards a New Past: Dissenting Essays in American History* (New York, 1967, 1968). Young is especially good in her assessments of the now bold, now cautious American policy in China and her estimate of the relative importance of political and economic factors in shaping U.S. policy. Other works helpful to me were Akira Iriye, *Across the Pacific: An Inner History of American-East Asian Relations* (New York, 1967); and Sandra C. Thomson (now Taylor), "Vicarious Imperialists: Americans and Japanese Expansionism, 1870-1880" (unpublished paper, 1970).

U.S.–Chinese relations have drawn the most attention among historians treating American policy toward the Far East. One should start with Michael Hunt's book, already cited. A broader, and excellent, synthesis is Warren I. Cohen, *America's Response to China: An Interpretative History of Sino-American Relations* (New York, 1971); and, focused on a more limited period, Paul A. Varg, *The Making of a Myth: The United States and China, 1897–1912* (East Lansing, 1968). John K. Fairbank recommends looking on U.S. concern with China as part of a general "European" outlook in " 'American China Policy' to 1898: A Misconception," *PHR* 39 (November 1970). Useful material is also available in Robert McClellan, *The Heathen Chinee: A Study of American Attitudes toward China, 1890–1905* (Columbus, 1970); and Curtis Henson, *Commissioners and Commodores: The East India Squadron and American Diplomacy in China* (University, Ala., 1982).

Students of the instruments of diplomacy have concentrated on the navy, but three excellent general works are Allan R. Millett and Peter Maslowski, *For the Common Defense: A Military History of the United States of America* (New York, 1984); Richard D. Challener, *Admirals, Generals, and American Foreign Policy, 1898–1914* (Princeton, 1973); and James L. Abrahamson, *America Arms for a New Century: The Making of a Great Military Power* (New York, 1981), an excellent analysis of how advancing military professionalism, combined with new technology and a changing world context, caused army and navy reformers to advocate building "war" rather than "peace" armies and navies.

William R. Braisted, *The United States Navy in the Pacific, 1897–1909* (Austin, 1958), is excellent on U.S. relations with other powers in China and revealing on much more than naval matters. For the navy "fit enough," I relied heavily on Lance C. Buhl's essay, "Maintaining 'An American Navy,' 1865–1889," in Kenneth J. Hagan, ed., *In Peace and War: Interpretations of American Naval History, 1775–1978* (Westport, 1978). Other recommended works on the navy are Robert Seager II, "Ten Years before Mahan: The Unofficial Case for the New Navy, 1880–1890," *MVHR* 40 (December 1953); Hagan, *American Gunboat Diplomacy and the Old Navy, 1897–1889* (Westport, 1973); and Walter R.

Herrick, *The American Naval Revolution* (Baton Rouge, 1966), which also helps untangle the Haitain and Chilean affairs of 1889–92. Two books on the hallmarks of an age ready to respond professionally to greater danger are Jeffrey M. Dorwart, *The Office of Naval Intelligence: The Birth of America's First Intelligence Agency, 1865–1918* (Annapolis, 1979), which demonstrates that the navy generally, not only the O.N.I., adopted its tougher view of the world from the late eighties onward; and the helpful if sparse Ronald Spector, *Professors of War: The Naval War College and the Development of the Naval Profession* (Newport, 1977). An anecdotal account is Robert Erwin Johnson, *Far China Station: The U.S. Navy in Asian Waters, 1800–1898* (Annapolis, 1979).

The army is best studied in Russell F. Weigley's *History of the United States Army* (enlarged ed., Bloomington, 1984). Little has yet been done on the diplomatic "corps" of the era, but see Charles O. Paullin, *Diplomatic Negotiations of American Naval Officers, 1778–1883* (Baltimore, 1912); and Richard Hume Werking, *The Master Architects: Building the United States Foreign Service, 1890–1913* (Lexington, Ky., 1977), a solid study of the establishment of a professional foreign service, a development more characteristic of the years after than before 1900. A bizarre, timely work, demonstrating Americans' awareness of international danger and desire to flex their muscles is Frank R. Stockton's satirical novel, *The Great War Syndicate* (New York, 1889); I am indebted to Marcus Cunliffe for bringing this to my attention.

Among the biographic studies that should be consulted are Glyndon G. Van Deusen, *William Henry Seward* (New York, 1967), though it is thin on foreign affairs; and Ernest N. Paolino, *The Foundations of the American Empire: William Henry Seward and U.S. Foreign Policy* (Ithaca, 1973). Though outdated in some respects, Allan Nevins, *Hamilton Fish: The Inner History of the Grant Administration*, 2 vols. (New York, 1936), is still pertinent. An able study of a minor but unjustly neglected figure is Joseph A. Fry, *Henry S. Sanford: Diplomacy in Nineteenth-Century America* (Reno, 1982), good on U.S. policy toward the Congo. Allan Peskin, *Garfield: A Biography* (Kent, 1978), is of little interest but contains the story about President Hayes's landlubber secretary of the navy. Very good on the politics and domestic context of naval reform and expansion is Benjamin Franklin Cooling, *Benjamin Franklin Tracy: Father of the Modern American Fighting Navy* (Hamden, Conn., 1973). Also valuable for naval-diplomatic history are the excellent Frederick C. Drake, *The Empire of the Seas: A Biography of Rear Admiral Robert Wilson Shufeldt, USN* (Honolulu, 1984); Robert Seager II, *Alfred Thayer Mahan: The Man and His Letters* (Annapolis, 1977); William E. Livezey, *Mahan on Sea Power* (Norman, 1947); Robert Seager II and Doris D. Maguire, eds., *Letters and Papers of Alfred Thayer Mahan* (Annapolis, 1975); and Ronald Spector, *Admiral of the New Empire: The Life and Career of George Dewey* (Baton Rouge, 1974), which, perhaps unavoidably, manages to render the hero of Manila a little ridiculous.

Studies of other policymakers include Michael J. Devine, *John W. Foster: Politics and Diplomacy in the Imperial Era, 1873–1917* (Athens, Ga., 1981); Bingham Duncan, *Whitelaw Reid: Journalist, Politician, Diplomat* (Athens, Ga., 1975); Gerald G. Eggert, *Richard Olney: Evolution of a Statesman* (University Park, Pa., 1974), which neglects all but the most important issues confronting Cleveland's last secretary of state; William C. Widenor, *Henry Cabot Lodge and the Search for an American Foreign Policy* (Berkeley, 1980), an intellectual biography; John A. Garraty, *Henry Cabot Lodge* (New York, 1953); Margaret Leech's thorough narrative, *In the Days of McKinley* (New York, 1959); H. Wayne Morgan, *William McKinley and His America* (Syracuse, 1963), which is disappointing compared to his excellent little book, *America's Road to Empire: The War with Spain and Overseas Expansion* (New York, 1965); and the solid but unsurprising Kenton J. Clymer, *John Hay: The Gentleman as Diplomat* (Ann Arbor, 1975), which is most interesting on the Boer War and the canal treaties and weakest on the policy relationship between Hay and McKinley. Excellent chapters on Seward, Fish, James G. Blaine, and Mahan by Gordon H. Warren, James B. Chapin, Lester D. Langley, and Kenneth J. Hagan, respectively, appear in the first volume of Frank J. Merli and Theodore A. Wilson, eds., *Makers of American Diplomacy,* 2 vols. (New York, 1974).

Historians write far less on the Seward-Grant-Fish era than on later years, but a number of their works are valuable. The leading work on the *Alabama* claims is now Adrian Cook, *The Alabama Claims: American Politics and Anglo-American Relations, 1865–1872* (Ithaca, 1975); but see also Maureen M. Robson, "The *Alabama* Claims and the Anglo-American Reconciliation, 1865–71," *Canadian Historical Review* 42 (March 1961), analyzing the circumstances that first delayed and then permitted a settlement; and Doris M. Dashew, "The Story of an Illusion: The Plan to Trade the *Alabama* Claims for Canada," *Civil War History* 15 (December 1969), good on Fish's working on and then abandoning the Canadian-annexation scheme. A sound work of narrative and analysis benefiting from use of Mexican sources is Thomas David Schoonover, *Dollars Over Dominion: The Triumph of Liberalism in Mexican-United States Relations, 1861–1867* (Baton Rouge, 1978), which reveals the ideological motives for opposing French intervention; a readable narrative is Alfred J. Hanna and Kathryn A. Hanna, *Napoleon III and Mexico: American Triumph over Monarchy* (Chapel Hill, 1971).

Much more work has recently been done on the Alaska purchase. Howard I. Kushner's *Conflict on the Northwest Coast: American-Russian Rivalry in the Pacific Northwest, 1790–1867* (Westport, 1975) focuses on the Russian side of the story; also valuable is Ronald J. Jensen, *The Alaska Purchase and Russian-American Relations* (Seattle, 1975); and Paul S. Holbo, *Tarnished Expansion: The Alaska Scan-*

dal, the Press, and Congress, 1867–1871 (Knoxville, 1983), which stresses the corruption story but does not fully persuade in seeing the scandal as a key in dampening enthusiasm for expansionism until the 1890s. Older works still valuable are F. A. Golder, "The Russian Fleet and the Civil War," *AHR* 20 (July 1915); Richard E. Welch, Jr., "American Public Opinion and the Purchase of Russian America," *American Slavic and East European Review* 17 (December 1958); and Thomas A. Bailey, "Why the United States Purchased Alaska," *PHR* 3 (February 1934), which should be read in conjunction with Kushner, "The Russian Fleet and the American Civil War: Another View," *Historian* 34 (August 1972).

An important new book is Richard H. Bradford, *The Virginius Affair* (Boulder, 1980), based on multiarchival work, which stresses Britain's help in bringing about a peaceful settlement. Anti-imperialist protests of this era are examined in Robert L. Beisner, "Thirty Years Before Manila: E. L. Godkin, Carl Schurz, and Anti-Imperialism in the Gilded Age," *Historian* 30 (August 1968).

On Blaine see the indispensable articles by Russell H. Bastert, "Diplomatic Reversal: Frelinghuysen's Opposition to Blaine's Pan-American Policy in 1882," *MVHR* 42 (March 1956), and "A New Approach to the Origins of Blaine's Pan American Policy," *HAHR* 39 (August 1959). Another important study helping to restore the 1881–82 interlude to respectful attention is David M. Pletcher's *The Awkward Years: American Foreign Relations under Garfield and Arthur* (Columbia, Mo., 1963). A competent synthesis is Justus D. Doenecke, *The Presidencies of James A. Garfield and Chester A. Arthur* (Lawrence, 1981).

A superb book, notable for its mastery of European issues, is Paul M. Kennedy, *The Samoan Tangle: A Study in Anglo-German-American Relations, 1878–1900* (Dublin, 1974). For more on the subject, see R. P. Gilson, *Samoa 1830 to 1900: The Politics of a Multi-Cultural Community* (Melbourne, 1970), centered on the Samoans themselves;

Sylvia Masterman, *The Origins of International Rivalry in Samoa, 1845–1884* (London, 1934); Ernest Andrade, "The Giant Samoan Hurricane of 1899," *Naval War College Review* 34 (January–February 1981); and Joseph W. Ellison, "The Partition of Samoa: A Study in Imperialism and Diplomacy," *PHR* 8 (September 1939). A surprising amount of work is being done on U.S.-Korean relations. Those interested in pursuing the matter further should consult the ponderous but thorough George Alexander Lensen, *Balance of Intrigue: International Rivalry in Korea & Manchuria, 1884–1899,* 2 vols. (Tallahassee, 1982); another plodding but thorough account, based on sources in oriental as well as western languages, Martina Deuchler, *Confucian Gentlemen and Barbarian Envoys: the Opening of Korea, 1875–1885* (Seattle, 1977); Robert R. Swartout, Jr., *Mandarins, Gunboats, and Power Politics: Owen Nickerson Denny and the International Rivalries in Korea* (Honolulu, 1980); Jeffrey M. Dorwart, "The Independent Minister: John M. B. Sill and the Struggle against Japanese Expansion in Korea, 1894–1897," *PHR* 44 (November 1975), fascinating on the theme of the field-to-center shift; Fred Harvey Harrington, *God, Mammon and the Japanese: Dr. Horace N. Allen and Korean-American Relations, 1884–1905* (Madison, 1961), and his "An American View of Korean-American Relations, 1882–1905" (unpublished paper, 1983); and Yur-Bok Lee, "A Korean View of Korean-American Relations, 1882–1905" (unpublished paper, 1982).

A fine article on an isolated 1885 incident in Panama, which the author sees as an imperialist precursor, is Daniel H. Wicks, "Dress Rehearsal: United States Intervention on the Isthmus of Panama, 1885," *PHR* 49 (November 1980). On the Bering Sea issue, see Charles S. Campbell, Jr., "The Anglo-American Crisis in the Bering Sea, 1890–1891," *MVHR* 48 (December 1961), and "The Bering Sea Settlements of 1892," *PHR* 32 (November 1963). Minor Mideastern matters are considered in William N. Still, Jr., *American Sea Power in the Old World: The United States Navy in*

European and Near Eastern Waters, 1865–1917 (Westport, 1980). Some of the domestic political issues referred to at the end of Chapter Two come from Joseph P. O'Grady's articles, "Religion and American Diplomacy: An Incident in Austro-American Relations," *American Jewish Historical Quarterly* 59 (June 1970), and "The Roman Question in American Politics: 1885," *Church and State* 10 (Autumn 1968).

A few items on intellectual developments underlying the paradigm shift should be mentioned: Frederick Jackson Turner, "The Significance of the Frontier in American History," *Annual Report of the American Historical Association for the Year 1893*; Robert C. Bannister, *Social Darwinism: Science and Myth in Anglo-American Social Thought* (Philadelphia, 1979), which mostly supersedes Richard Hofstadter's *Social Darwinism in American Thought, 1860–1915* (Philadelphia, 1945); Donald C. Bellomy, "Social Darwinism Revisited," *Perspectives in American History*, New Series, I, 1984, pp. 1–129, which may in turn have superseded Bannister; Dorothea R. Muller, "Josiah Strong and American Nationalism: A Reevaluation," *JAH* 53 (December 1966); and Stuart Anderson, *Race and Rapprochement: Anglo-Saxonism and Anglo-American Relations, 1895–1904* (Rutherford, N.J., 1981).

Other works on the Harrison administration are A. T. Volwiler, "Harrison, Blaine, and American Foreign Policy, 1889–1893," *American Philosophical Society Proceedings* 79 (1938), old but essential; Allan B. Spetter, "Harrison and Blaine: Foreign Policy, 1889–1893," *Indiana Magazine of History* 65 (September 1969); and David M. Pletcher, "Reciprocity and Latin America in the Early 1890s: A Foretaste of Dollar Diplomacy," *PHR* 47 (February 1978). The first monograph on the Chilean fracas is Joyce S. Goldberg, *The Baltimore Affair: United States Relations with Chile, 1891–1892* (Lincoln, 1986), which I was able to read in manuscript. In addition, see Frederick B. Pike, *Chile and the United States, 1880–1962* (Notre Dame, Ind., 1963); Francis

X. Holbrook and John Nikol, "The Chilean Crisis of 1891–1892," *American Neptune* 38 (October 1978), an indictment of Chile and defense of Secretary of the Navy Tracy; Goldberg, "Patrick Egan: Irish-American Minister to Chile, 1889–93," *Eire-Ireland* 14 (Fall 1979); and Harold Blackemore, *British Nitrates and Chilean Politics, 1886–1898: Balmaceda and North* (London, 1974).

Standard, older works on Hawaii in the Harrison-Cleveland period still qualifying as required reading include Julius W. Pratt, *Expansionists of 1898: The Acquisition of Hawaii and the Spanish Islands* (Baltimore, 1936); William A. Russ, Jr., *The Hawaiian Revolution (1893–94)* (Selinsgrove, Pa., 1959); and Merze Tate, *The United States & The Hawaiian Kingdom, A Political History* (New Haven, 1965). An important study of the resistance to Hawaiian annexation and Cleveland's abandonment of the project is Thomas J. Osborne, *"Empire Can Wait": American Opposition to Hawaiian Annexation, 1893-1898* (Kent, 1981); readers should watch their step, however, for this book is strewn with fallen straw men. For Harrison's lack of enthusiasm for annexation, see George W. Baker, Jr., "Benjamin Harrison and Hawaiian Annexation: A Reinterpretation," *PHR* 33 (August 1964). See also Michael J. Devine, "John W. Foster and the Struggle for the Annexation of Hawaii," ibid., 46 (February 1977); and Hugh B. Hammett, "The Cleveland Administration and Anglo-American Naval Friction in Hawaii, 1893–1894," *Military Affairs* 40 (February 1976).

Little work exists on Cleveland and the Far East, but see Jeffrey M. Dorwart, *The Pigtail War: American Involvement in the Sino-Japanese War of 1894–1895* (Amherst, 1975), an unpretentious account that may overstate Secretary of State Gresham's ineptness. On the Brazilian rebellion, first see Lawrence F. Hill, *Diplomatic Relations Between the United States and Brazil* (Durham, 1932). For the "markets" approach, consult Walter LaFeber's "United States Depression Diplomacy and the Brazilian Revolution,

1893–1894," *HAHR* 40 (February 1960). The most persuasive works, however, are Charles W. Calhoun, "American Policy Toward the Brazilian Revolt of 1893–94: A Reexamination," *DH* 4 (Winter 1980), excellently grounded in the sources; and James F. Vivian, "United States Policy during the Brazilian Naval Revolt, 1893–94: The Case for American Neutrality," *American Neptune* 41 (October 1981).

On the Venezuelan crisis of 1895–96, an important early work is Nelson M. Blake, "Background of Cleveland's Venezuela Policy," *AHR* 47 (January 1942). The British perspective is available in John A. S. Grenville's *Lord Salisbury and Foreign Policy: The Close of the Nineteenth Century* (London, 1964). A book of surprisingly little value for the student of American policy is Miriam Hood, *Gunboat Diplomacy, 1895–1905: Great Power Pressure in Venezuela* (London, 1983). One of the better works on Cleveland's drift toward intervention in Cuba is Margaret E. Kless, "The Second Grover Cleveland Administration and Cuba: A Study of Policy and Motivation, 1895–1897" (M.A. thesis, The American University, 1970).

Still important on the history of the Spanish-American War is French Ensor Chadwick, *The Relations of the United States and Spain: The Spanish-American War*, 2 vols. (New York, 1911). Ernest R. May, *Imperial Democracy: The Emergence of America as a Great Power* (New York, 1961), though adhering to the view that McKinley was pushed into war by public hysteria, is helpful in interpreting the last few weeks of negotiations. David F. Trask, *The War with Spain in 1898* (New York, 1981), is now the best military history and informative as well on diplomatic decisions, though underestimating McKinley's readiness to use military power for political goals. Other general accounts deserving close reading are Lewis L. Gould, *The Spanish-American War and President McKinley* (Lawrence, 1982); Philip S. Foner, *The Spanish-Cuban-American War and the Birth of American Imperialism, 1895–1902*, 2 vols. (New York, 1972), which argues that the Cuban rebels could have won without

American help and would have preferred to do so; and the well written, if uneven, new popular account, G. J. A. O'Toole, *The Spanish War: An American Epic–1898* (New York, 1984). See also the widely consulted dissertation, John L. Offner, "President McKinley and the Origins of the Spanish-American War" (Pennsylvania State University, 1957).

Particular issues related to the origins and prosecution of the war can be explored in Louis A. Pérez, Jr., "Cuba between Empires, 1898–1899," *PHR* 48 (November 1979), excellent on the Cuban insurgents' reaction to U.S. intervention; Julius W. Pratt, "The 'Large Policy' of 1898," *MVHR* 19 (September 1932), portraying the impact of the imperialist "clique"; H. Wayne Morgan, "The DeLôme Letter: A New Appraisal," *Historian* 26 (November 1963); Hyman G. Rickover, *How the Battleship "Maine" Was Destroyed* (Washington, D.C., 1976), which supports the view that an internal explosion, probably caused by a fire in a coal bunker, destroyed the ship; John L. Offner, "McKinley's Final Attempts to Avoid War with Spain" (unpublished paper, 1984), which explores McKinley's use of a Vatican backchannel in trying to prevent war; John A. S. Grenville, "American Naval Preparations for War with Spain, 1896–1898," *Journal of American Studies* 2 (April 1968); and Offner, "The United States and France: Ending the Spanish-American War," *DH* 7 (Winter 1983), which shows McKinley very much in charge of the armistice negotiations.

The subject of American imperialism continues to attract the attention of scholars. A significant study is Ernest R. May, *American Imperialism: A Speculative Essay* (New York, 1968), an impressive effort flawed by an excessively narrow definition of "imperialism"; May attempts to refine the concept of public opinion, trace the influence of European fashions on American views, and determine why the United States rejected "imperialism" in the 1870s, adopted it in 1898, and then abruptly dropped it again shortly thereafter. See also the enormously suggestive essay, James A. Field, Jr., " 'American Imperialism': The Worst Chapter in Almost Any Book," with commentary by Walter LaFeber and Robert L. Beisner, *AHR* 83 (June 1978). Field is reluctant to accept the imperialist consequences of American policy, but his essay is valuable for its penetrating assault on the "markets" thesis and intriguing assessment of the relationships among diplomacy, naval developments, and the building of ocean cable networks. Another traditionally oriented work is Goran Rystad, *Ambiguous Imperialism: American Foreign Policy and Domestic Politics at the Turn of the Century* (Lund, Sweden, 1975), focusing on the reciprocal relationship between foreign policy and domestic politics, a theme that should also be explored through William E. Leuchtenburg, "Progressivism and Imperialism: The Progressive Movement and American Foreign Policy, 1898–1916," *MVHR* 39 (December 1952). A graceful if unfocused essay on the cultural significance of the Spanish-American War and imperialism, influenced by Robert Wiebe's *Search for Order,* is Gerald F. Linderman, *The Mirror of War: American Society and the Spanish-American War* (Ann Arbor, 1974). Also relevant are Walter L. Williams, "United States Indian Policy and the Debate over Philippine Annexation: Implications for the Origins of American Imperialism" *JAH* 66 (March 1980); and Whitney T. Perkins, *Denial of Empire: The United States and Its Dependencies* (Leyden, 1962).

The decision finally to annex Hawaii should first be examined through three older works: William A. Russ, Jr., *The Hawaiian Republic (1894–98) and Its Struggle To Win Annexation* (Selinsgrove, Pa., 1961); S. K. Stevens, *American Expansion in Hawaii, 1842–1898* (Harrisburg, 1945); and Merze Tate, *Hawaii: Reciprocity or Annexation* (East Lansing, 1968). See also Tate, "Great Britain and the Sovereignty of Hawaii," *PHR* 31 (November 1962); William Michael Morgan, "The Anti-Japanese Origins of the Hawaiian Annexation Treaty of 1897," *DH* 6 (Winter 1982); and Thomas J. Osborne, "Trade or War? America's Annexation of Hawaii Reconsidered," *PHR* 50 (August 1981).

A fascinating primary source on the peace negotiations, and especially on the decision to demand the cession of the Philippines, is H. Wayne Morgan, ed., *Making Peace with Spain: The Diary of Whitelaw Reid, September–December, 1898* (Austin, 1965). Also revealing on acquiring the Philippines is Paolo E. Coletta, "McKinley, the Peace Negotiations, and the Acquisition of the Philippines," *PHR* 30 (November 1961), an excellent summary of how McKinley got the United States firmly lodged in the archipelago weeks before the Paris peace talks; and Coletta's "Bryan, McKinley and the Treaty of Paris," ibid. 26 (May 1957). For foreign complications, see articles by James K. Eyre, Jr., "Japan and the American Annexation of the Philippines," ibid. 11 (March 1942), and "Russia and the American Acquisition of the Philippines," *MVHR* 28 (March 1942); and Thomas A. Bailey, "Dewey and the Germans at Manila Bay," *AHR* 45 (October 1939). Peter W. Stanley, *A Nation in the Making: The Philippines and the United States, 1899–1921* (Cambridge, Mass., 1974) is also interesting.

For McKinley's strong leadership in both war and diplomacy, see Lewis L. Gould, *The Presidency of William McKinley* (Lawrence, 1980), the zenith of McKinley revisionism. The president's role in shaping public opinion is explored in a significant new study that undermines the common assumption that the executive branch usually responds *to* public opinion, Robert C. Hilderbrand, *Power and the People: Executive Management of Public Opinion in Foreign Affairs, 1897–1921* (Chapel Hill, 1981). Other important works reversing the traditional image of McKinley include Gould, "William McKinley and the Expansion of Presidential Power," *Ohio History* 87 (Winter 1978); Paul S. Holbo, "Presidential Leadership in Foreign Affairs: William McKinley and the Turpie-Foraker Amendment," *AHR* 72 (July 1967); and Joseph A. Fry, "William McKinley and the

Coming of the Spanish-American War: A Study of the Besmirching and Redemption of an Historical Image," *DH* 3 (Winter 1979), which summarizes the historiography. George S. Boutwell's remark on McKinley's determination to annex the Philippines appears in Thomas H. Brown, "George Sewall Boutwell: Public Servant (1818–1905)" (Ph.D. dissertation, New York University, 1979).

On the U.S.–Philippine War, readers for years had little to consult except Leon Wolff, *Little Brown Brother* (Garden City, 1961). This popular and not always accurate account has been succeeded by a number of works, especially Richard E. Welch, Jr.'s *Response to Imperialism: The United States and the Philippine-American War, 1899–1902* (Chapel Hill, 1979), an excellent but unnecessarily brief analysis. Welch's book should be read along with the more passionate book by Stuart Creighton Miller, *"Benevolent Assimilation": The American Conquest of the Philippines, 1899–1903* (New Haven, 1982), a thoroughgoing indictment of the U.S. Army's actions. Other recommended works are David Haward Bain, *Sitting in Darkness: Americans in the Philippines* (Boston, 1984), a popular account that also traces the long-term effects of American imperialism to the Philippines of Ferdinand Marcos; and Grania Bolton, "Military Diplomacy and National Liberation: Insurgent-American Relations After the Fall of Manila," *Military Affairs* 36 (October 1972). Filipino and American casualties, as well as the issue of U.S. atrocities, are explored in John M. Gates, "War-Related Deaths in the Philippines, 1898–1902," *PHR* 53 (August 1984), and Richard E. Welch, Jr., "American Atrocities in the Philippines: The Indictment and the Response," ibid. 43 (May 1974), both precise and careful analyses. Trying to answer a question whose answer is normally taken for granted is Glenn A. May, "Why the United States Won the Philippine-American War, 1899–1902," ibid. 52 (November 1983). One reason for the eventual U.S. victory was collaboration on the part of Filipinos, explored in May's "Filipino Resistance to American Occupation: Batangas, 1899–1902," ibid. 48 (November 1979), and Norman G. Owen, "Winding Down the War in Albay, 1900–1903," ibid.

Those interested in anti-imperialism might still begin with Fred H. Harrington's convenient summary, "The Anti-Imperialist Movement in the United States, 1898–1900," *MVHR* 22 (September 1935). For richer accounts see Robert L. Beisner, *Twelve Against Empire: The Anti-Imperialists, 1898–1900* (New York, 1968; with new preface, Chicago, 1985), which finds both the strengths and weaknesses of the anti-imperialist movement in its traditionalism and elitism; Beisner, "1898 and 1968: The Anti-Imperialists and the Doves," *Political Science Quarterly* 85 (June 1978), which compares the movement with the anti-Vietnam War protests; E. Berkeley Tompkins, *Anti-Imperialism in the United States: The Great Debate, 1890–1920* (Philadelphia, 1970), a valuable survey of the facts which, however, portrays the anti-imperialists without their warts; and Daniel B. Schirmer, *Republic or Empire: American Resistance to the Philippine War* (Cambridge, Mass., 1972), a vigorous, present-minded narrative of Boston anti-imperialism saddled with the unconvincing thesis that anti-imperialism represented a struggle of the old mercantile elite, joined by labor, Negroes, and "youth" against imperialist bankers and manufacturers. Other interesting works on anti-imperialism include Richard E. Welch, Jr.'s "Motives and Policy Objectives of Anti-Imperialists, 1898," *Mid-America* 51 (April 1969), and "Organized Religion and the Philippine-American War, 1899–1902," *Mid-America* 55 (July 1973); Goran Rystad, "Ambiguous Anti-Imperialism: American Expansionism and Its Critics at the Turn of the Century," in Marc Chénetier and Rob Kroes, eds., *Impressions of a Gilded Age: The American Fin de Siecle* (Amsterdam, 1983); Christopher Lasch, "The Anti-Imperialists, the Philippines, and the Inequality of Man," *Journal of Southern History* 24 (August 1958); and Philip S. Foner and Richard C. Winchester, eds., *The Anti-Imperialist Reader: A Documentary History of Anti-Imperialism in the United States. Volume I: From the Mexi-*

can War to the Election of 1900 (New York, 1984), an excellent collection of primary sources.

For the Open Door notes, I learned much from Thomas J. McCormick, *China Market: America's Quest for Informal Empire, 1893–1901* (Chicago, 1967), an intriguing account of economic expansionism in China and its bearing on U.S. decisions on the Philippines; this book suffers, however, from an underestimation of ideological and irrational influences. A brief version of some of McCormick's arguments appears in his "Insular Imperialism and the Open Door: The China Market and the Spanish-American War," *PHR* 32 (May 1963). Excellent on the influence of the exporters' and investors' communities is Charles S. Campbell, Jr., *Special Business Interests and the Open Door Policy* (New Haven, 1951). Michael H. Hunt, *Frontier Defense and the Open Door: Manchuria in Chinese-American Relations, 1895–1911* (New Haven, 1973), depicts Hay as less certain yet more ambitious in his goals than I do. Contrasting versions of how the Open Door policy evolved in the early years of the twentieth century appear in Raymond A. Esthus, "The Changing Concept of the Open Door, 1899–1910," *MVHR* 46 (December 1959); and Ian J. Bickerton, "John Hay's Open Door Policy: A Re-examination," *Australian Journal of Politics and History* 33 (April 1977). See also Paul A. Varg, "William Woodville Rockhill and the Open Door Notes," *Journal of Modern History* 24 (December 1952), who thinks Hay was attempting to undermine spheres of influence in the first note; and Michael H. Hunt, "Americans in the China Market: Economic Opportunities and Economic Nationalism, 1890's–1931," *Business History Review* 51 (Fall 1977).

Besides works already cited, aspects of the rapprochement with Britain can be followed in Charles S. Campbell, Jr., "Anglo-American Relations, 1897–1901," in Paolo E. Coletta, ed., *Threshold to American Internationalism: Essays on the Foreign Policies of William McKinley* (New York, 1970); Stuart Anderson, "Racist Anglo-Saxonism and the American Response to the Boer War," *DH* 2 (Summer 1978); Thomas J. Noer, *Briton, Boer, and Yankee: The United States and South Africa, 1870–1914* (Kent, 1978); and John H. Ferguson, *American Diplomacy and the Boer War* (Philadelphia, 1939). For the issue of imperialism in McKinley's reelection, see Walter LaFeber, "The Election of 1900," in Arthur M. Schlesinger, Jr., and Fred L. Israel, eds., *History of American Presidential Elections* (New York, 1971), vol. 3; which supersedes Thomas A. Bailey, "Was the Presidential Election of 1900 a Mandate on Imperialism?" *MVHR* 24 (June 1937).

SUBJECT INDEX

Adams, Brooks, 13, 20, 81, 121
Adams, Charles Francis, 29, 42, 45
Adams, Henry, 6
Adams, John Quincy, 54
Addams, Jane, 139
Africa, 9, 15, 64, 71, 82, 91, 92, 114
Aguinaldo, Emilio, 130, 133, 135, 136, 140, 149
Alabama claims controversy, 4, 5, 6, 27, 38–42, 44, 51, 170
Alaska, 41, 45
  annexation of, 46–48, 171
  boundary dispute (with Canada), 143
Alexander II, Czar of Russia, 47
Alger, Russell, 93
Allison, William B., 121
ambassador, rank of, 29, 90
American Asiatic Association, 137
American Mission, 4, 9–10, 83–84, 140
Anglophobia, 6, 111, 113, 143
Anglo-Saxonism, 82
Angola, 98
anti-imperialists and anti-imperialism, 4–5, 50, 92, 97, 131, 136, 139–40, 141, 142, 143, 146, 149, 156, 180
Argentina, 56, 99, 102
Armenia, 86, 112, 113
Army, U.S., 7–8, 58, 79, 89, 90, 134, 138, 140–41, 150, 179
Arthur, Chester A. (Arthur administration), 8, 19, 56, 58, 59, 64, 65, 86, 157
Asia (Far East), 11, 15, 17, 19, 21, 23, 28, 30, 32, 44, 60, 64, 81, 82, 84, 87, 94, 95, 97, 105, 107, 114,

121, 131, 132, 137, 140, 142, 143, 144, 149, 150, 152, 155, 157, 166
  new policy for (ca. 1895), 91, 92, 144, 145
  See also specific countries
Austria-Hungary, 20, 46, 69
Azores Islands, 98

Babcock, Orville, Gen., 49
Bahamas, 45
Balmaceda, José Manuel, 101, 102
Banks, Nathaniel, 40
Bayard, Thomas F., 11
Bechuanaland, 114
Belgium, 114
  beliefs and traditions, 9–12
Bering Sea disputes (1886–1893), 62–63, 104
Berlin conference (1884), 19, 64
Berlin Treaty (1884), 64
Black Sea Treaty, 4
Blaine, James G., 27, 44, 96, 97, 157
  Haiti and, 98
  Hawaii and, 27
  hemispheric policy of, 54–57, 99
  New Orleans incident (1891) and, 100
  Valparaiso Crisis (1891–1892) and, 100–3
  War of the Pacific (1879–1884) and, 55–56, 101
  See also Pan-American conferences
Blount, James H., 105
Boer Republic. *See* South Africa
Boer War, 142, 143, 170
Bolivia, 55

AUTHOR INDEX

193

*From the Old Diplomacy to the New,
1865–1900, Second Edition,* was copy-edited
by Terrance Stanton. Production editor was
B. W. Barrett. The book was composed by
The Four Corners Press and printed and
bound by Thomson-Shore, Inc.